London's Country Buses

387 ALDBURY &
TRING
SMM 15F

London's Country Buses

John A. Gray AM Inst TA

LONDON
IAN ALLAN LTD

First published 1980

ISBN 0 7110 0963 5

Published by Ian Allan Ltd, Shepperton, Surrey; and printed by Ian Allan Printing Ltd at their works at Coombelands in Runnymede, England

Other transport books by the same author

London Buses in Camera
London's Suburban Buses
London's City Buses

Contents

Introduction and Acknowledgements 6

Gravesend 8

Dartford 13

The Near South-East 20

West Kent 23

West Sussex 25

East Surrey and Croydon 33

Redhill and Reigate 38

Green in Red 47

Country Life Ended 52

Red Connections: South-West 54

Western North Downs 60

Western Thames-Side 63

Bygone Slough 76

In the Chiltern Hundreds 80

Rickmansworth and Watford 90

St Albans and Beyond 98

Towns New and Old:
Stevenage and Hitchin 107

Bygone Barnet 116

Hertford, and into Essex 118

The Detached East 124

Introduction and Acknowledgements

Mention a London bus, and the mind pictures a red double-decker. But something like one seventh of the road fleet was painted green for the Country bus and Green Line coach fleet. After the noise and bustle depicted in *London's City Buses*, this album turns to the rather quieter and calmer life of the green buses in the home counties surrounding the metropolis.

Not that the green ones don't have their hectic moments. Some, on Green Line service, penetrate the core of London. And many of London's surrounding towns are so large as to require a network of close headway town routes. The gradual creep of straightened and widened roads, street lighting and traffic management notions means that the green bus route map contains progressively fewer leafy lanes and rustic scenes as they give way to intensified crop cultivation to verge edge, yellow lines and mock Georgian infills in our villages. Inclusion in this album of earlier scenes will nudge the memory. This *Country* book completes the trilogy which started with *London's Suburban Buses* in 1976.

Two bus operating areas were introduced by the London Passenger Transport Board in 1933; the Central Area whose buses were in the familiar mainly red livery, and the Country Area whose buses and coaches eventually settled in a mainly dark, or Lincoln, green.

The Country Area started life as an approximate outer band circumjacent to the developing further suburbs within the Central Area. Despite occasional expansion and contraction, it has retained its general shape ever since, though from the beginning of 1970, ownership was transferred from London Transport to the National Bus Company, and the Country Department of LT became London Country Bus Services Ltd. The area included large tracts of countryside in Kent, Surrey, Buckinghamshire, Hertfordshire and Essex, and small parts of Berkshire, Middlesex and Bedfordshire. Many market towns, within increasingly easy reach by rail to central London, were expanding in the interwar period, and the united bus operations under the LPTB provided services both within these growing towns and between them. Routes between the villages and towns were put on a more consolidated footing and passenger traffic developed as a result. The bus use story since then is by now familiar: virtually no car travel during the war years meant a huge reliance on stretched bus services. The 1945 feeling of relief seemed to encourage in huge numbers of people the desire to travel — not great distances, just far enough to visit a friend or beauty spot not seen during the dark years. Then came the decline in bus use proportionate to the increase in car ownership, and more recently, a stemming of the ebb tide, with some route restructuring, some financial help from local authorities and, not least, a younger fleet of vehicles, a broad range of which is shown here.

Nostalgic feelings for the prewar decade are currently prevalent, and so I make no excuse for including a large proportion of pictures taken in this period. One or two favourites I may have left out, for which I'm sorry. Other favourites appear more often

Above: Mooove over: Country conflict. / *LCBS*

perhaps than they fairly should; for those readers whose favourites they were, they are their bonus.

Acknowledgements

Again I thank the many photographers and photograph collectors for their patience and help in dealing with my requests. Those whose pictures appear in the book will, I hope, think that the publisher and I have done justice to their efforts. Much caption material was supplied, all of it in good faith, I'm sure, and where possible it has been checked.
Special thanks go to C. Carter, John Fielder, D. W. K. Jones, Tom Maddocks, Tom Moore and John Unwin. The staff of LCBS at the Reigate headquarters were very helpful and I'm pleased to include some of the company's photographs. Sandra continues to tolerate, even encourage, her husband's eccentricities in pursuing photographic records of the London Bus. And I offer thanks to the publisher's staff who will surely do as good a job on this title as they did for the first of the trilogy.

John A. Gray
Cambridge, June 1979

Gravesend

Top left: As the newly formed London Passenger Transport Board took over the operators within its area mostly during the 18 months from 1 July 1933, many acquired vehicles were despatched to places distant from their earlier homes. This first example was a little GMC, which came from Albanian to Northfleet garage. Many small operators used cheap American chassis for local buses. Their life was short. This one, in dark red with bright red waistband, did not survive long enough to be repainted into Country bus colours. / *D. W. K. Jones*

Bottom left: As though to disprove the earlier statement, this Leyland Lioness LTB1 model, the only one of its kind taken into LT stock, stayed close to home. Coming from Harris of Northfleet, it survived on Gravesend local services into 1935. /*D. W. K. Jones*

Above: A high-stepping gentleman alights from the rear of a Leyland Lion. This toughly built bus served its successive owners — London, Midland & Scottish Railway; London General Country Services, and LT — very well. LT concentrated most of the type at Northfleet garage, not far from which this shot was taken in February 1935. Route 497 about 45 years ago . . . / *D. W. K. Jones*

Below: . . . and much nearer today. Another Leyland product,albeit from a vastly reconstituted manufacturer, runs on a rather longer route 497 in the Gravesend area. SNB333 crosses from Darnley Road into Bath Road outside *The Wheatsheaf.* / *John A. Gray*

Left: London Transport never allocated standard length production Routemaster buses to the Country Area, and so none of that variety came to be taken into London Country's stock in 1970. However the longer version bus did, and a sizeable batch still worked from Northfleet garage in 1978.

RML2329 has come from Dartford on the frequent route 480 and here winks left to join Gravesend's one-way system at Bath Street. / *John A. Gray*

Below: Routemaster coach RMC1490 was decked out in an insurance advertiser's artwork in July 1973 at a time when it was both fashionable and remunerative for a bus operator to sell such mobile advertising space. The former Green Line coach brightens Gravesend's clock tower as it passes by on a local bus route. / *Edward Shirras*

Right: Route 490A was introduced as a new number early in 1972 when cuts in services were made around Longfield. Subsequent route numbering policy was to eliminate the suffix letter. From July 1973, more route changes in the area led to using 489 again. RF182, one of the face-lifted AEC Regal IV Green Line coaches, works on the short lived route, past rebuilding work for a bank in Longfield, in June 1973. Two years later this smart vehicle was to be disposed for scrap. / *Edward Shirras*

Below right: A narrow bodied version of the lightweight underfloor engined Bristol LHS took over many routes from RFs where narrow roads were encountered. BN27 shows how narrow the road is in Southfleet. The bus, pictured in October 1974, soon after delivery, has glazing edged by grey rubber, giving a light appearance. / *London Country Bus Services Ltd*

ASH WHITE SWAN
490A Southfleet Longfield
PAY AS YOU ENTER PLEASE
MLL 569
BARCLAYS
CONSTRUCTION COMPANY LIMITED

490
NEW ASH GREEN &
LONGFIELD STATION
XPD 127N

Right: AEC Reliance 6U2R model with Plaxton 49-seat coachwork, RS32, leaves New Road for Bath Street, Gravesend, in July 1978, on Green Line's then new route, 726. The indicator shows the southern orbital route's variation from the established 725 — 'via Heathrow' — in lettering so small as to be unreadable on distant approach. / *John A. Gray*

Below: Scottish-built Alexander coachwork on AEC Swift chassis goes to make up SMA10, once a comfortable Green Line coach, but by summer 1978, working a very local Gravesend bus route. Laden shoppers will have excellent visibility through the SMA's enormous windows, on their way up to Pepper Hill estate. / *John A. Gray*

Bottom: AEC Merlin MBS421 turns left outside *The Wheatsheaf* into Darnley Road in 1977. The Metro-Cammell bodywork has room for nearly as many standing passengers (27) as seated (33). / *John A. Gray*

Dartford

Above: Far from its native heath, this Leyland Lion, registered in Derby as were all London, Midland & Scottish Railway buses, spent all its previous working life in LMS ownership in the Boxmoor area. It ended its days in the Dartford-Gravesend sector, about as far from Hertfordshire as it could be sent within LT boundaries. Here it is at Dartford in London General Country Services' red, in August 1933. / *D. W. K. Jones*

Left: Photographed at Dartford while showing the 486 destination Denton, past Gravesend, this Maidstone & District Leyland Titan was still in its former owner's sage green and white livery in September 1933. 'General' transfers had been applied, though. Later this bus became TD161, and later still saw war service in the Liverpool Corporation fleet of former London Titans. / *D. W. K. Jones*

Left: By July 1978, the same route number, 486, was worked in Dartford by SM468, here sweeping round the corner outside the library in Market Street. The Swifts at Dartford garage were rather isolated from the rest of their kind at this time; the others were sprinkled about the western area between Leatherhead and Stevenage. / *John A. Gray*

Centre left: AEC Regent STL976 pauses at Crayford in March 1949 to allow a lady passenger to alight through the front doorway. The front staircase panel behind the driver's cab was glazed. / *D. W. K. Jones*

Below: Twenty two years later route 467 has the predictable RT, bound for Horton Kirby. By the time of this June 1971 photograph (at Wilmington), the motif adopted by LCBS had been applied to RT4050 to its staircase side panel. / *Tom Maddocks*

Right: Green Rover go-anywhere day bus tickets were being advertised at eight shillings (40p) by RT1021 in September 1970, a few months before decimal coinage came in. The suffixed route number 401A has disappeared from the Bexleyheath area too, consumed by the current practice influenced by computer requirements of redesignating such variants to the master number or a near, or 'rhyming', neighbour. / *Tom Maddocks*

Below right: Master route 401 entertained Swift SM524 at Dartford in March 1972. The one-man crew prepares his ticket machine in the still quite new bus. / *Tom Maddocks*

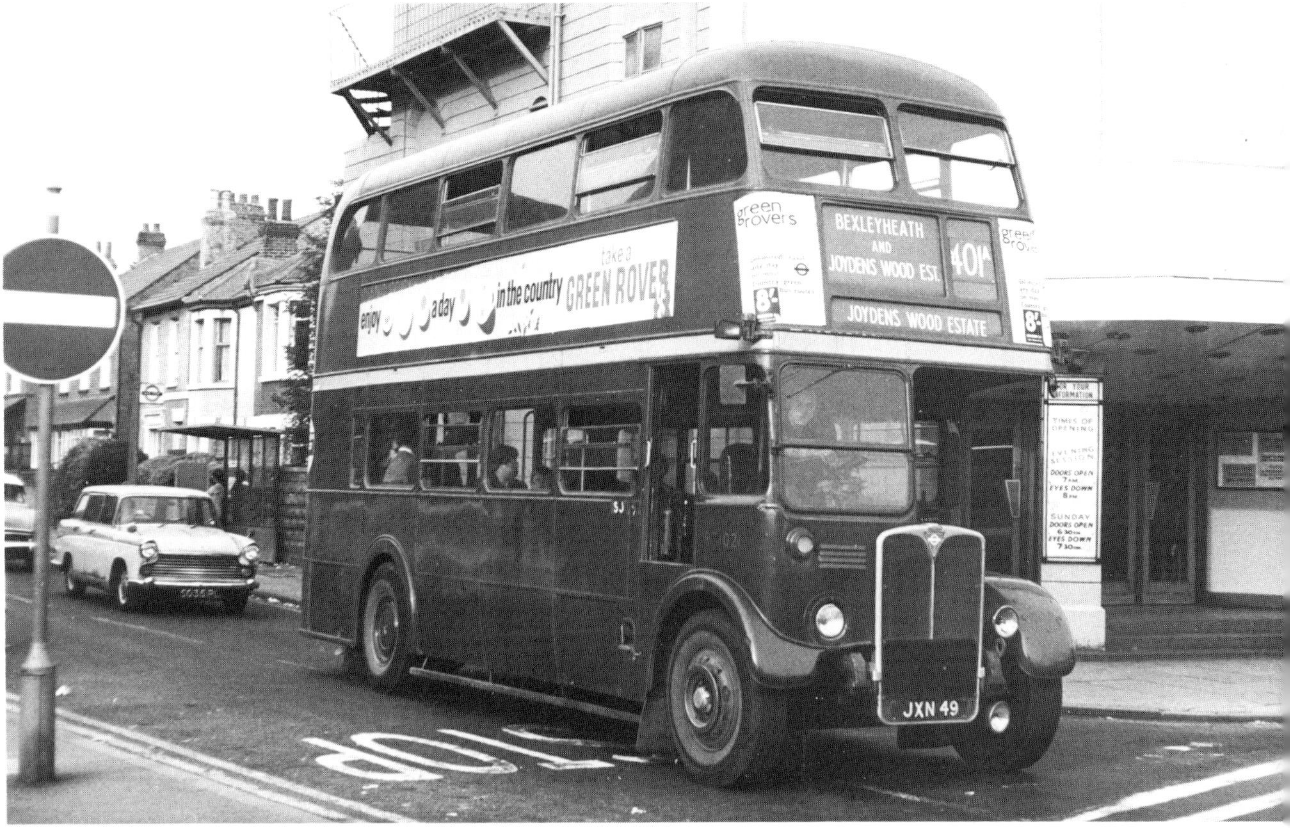

green rovers
BEXLEYHEATH AND JOYDENS WOOD EST.
401A
JOYDENS WOOD ESTATE
enjoy a day in the country
take a GREEN ROVER
JXN 49
STOP

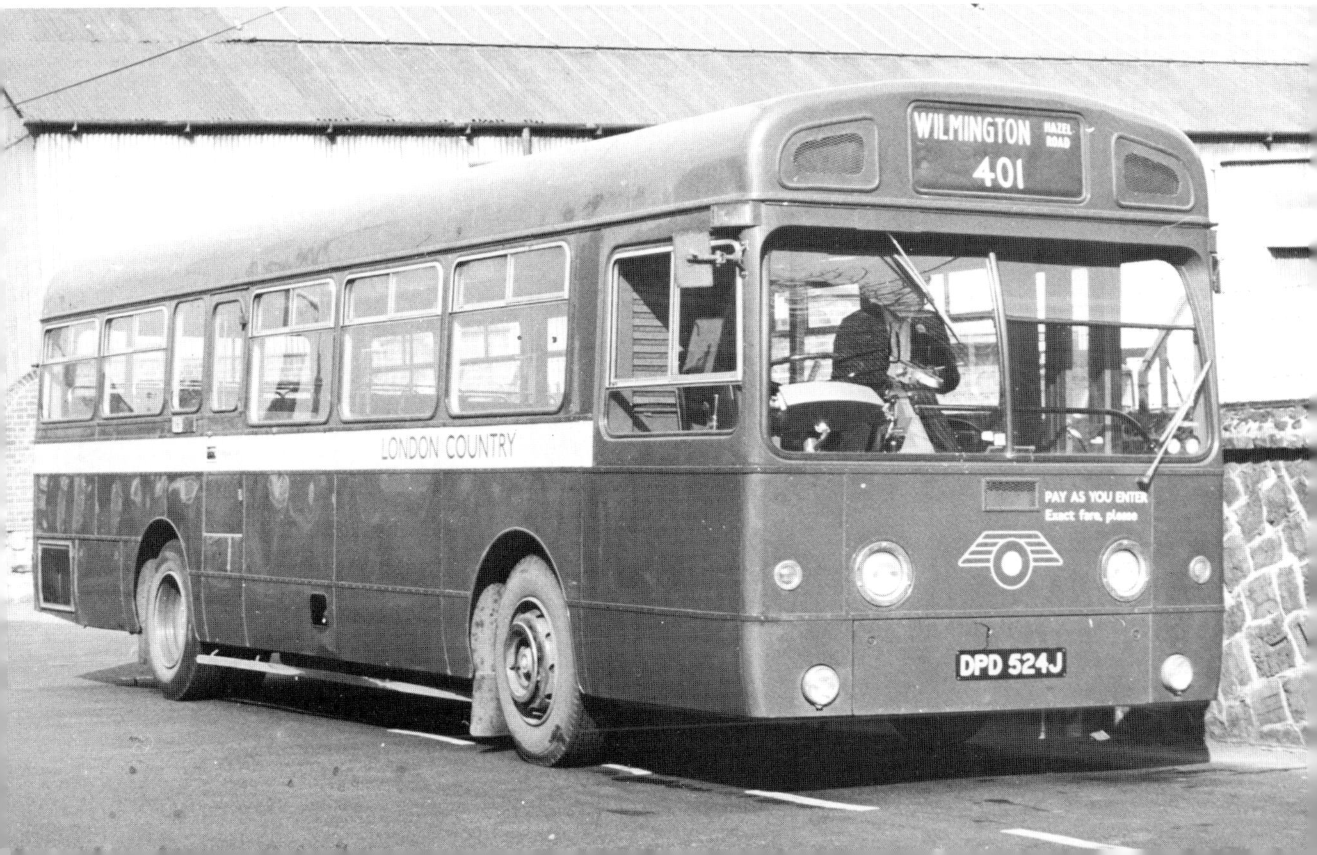

WILMINGTON HAZEL ROAD
401
LONDON COUNTRY
PAY AS YOU ENTER
Exact fare, please
DPD 524J

Left: Drinks for a thirsty mate arrive by SMA13. / *John A. Gray*

Below: RML2338 comes in to Market Street stop on route 480 past a driver climbing into his red RT on trolleybus-replaced route 96 in September 1971. / *Tom Maddocks*

Right: Long Routemasters continued to be the mainstay of busy route 480 in the summer of 1978. Some of them looked rather neglected; RML2336 had bonnet and wings in one shade of green, bodywork in another and National style grey wheels. / *John A. Gray*

Below right: For several years from mid-1974, London Country suffered from a shortage of serviceable buses. To ameliorate the ensuing difficulties, the company hired vehicles from six operators for varying periods. It might seem appropriate for fellow members of the National Bus Company to provide vehicles for hire, but in the event only one — Western National — did so. Four of the operators were local authority transport departments (the sixth being London Transport), one of which was Maidstone Borough Council whose Leyland Titan PD2As helped out from Dartford garage for about 10 months in 1975-76. / *LCBS*

MORE WIN MORE on LITTLEWOODS
LONDON COUNTRY
RML 2336
CUV 336C

499
DARTFORD
BUILDERS
JOINERS
SWALE GAS CALOR MAIN DEALER
SIGNWRITERS
517 RKR

Above: By summertime 1978, repainted SM492 was working on route 499 (the highest route number in the original south of Thames series) at same spot as Maidstone's light blue Titan a couple of years earlier. Coincidentally the Phase Two Leyland National SNB273 shows 400, the lowest route number in the series, and used previously at Slough. / *John A. Gray*

Below: This Reliance coach, P9, had been in LCBS ownership for only two months when photographed in Market Street. Since 1973, a fleet of 12 similar Plaxton-bodied coaches has been built up, some new, some secondhand, to allow LCBS to enter the market for luxury coach hire and excursions. All of them have the huge volume 12.5 litre AEC engine. / *John A. Gray*

Right: RT3886 has come south-west from Dartford and here picks up some heavily clothed passengers in February 1971 from the joint bus and coach stop by Sidcup LT garage, actually at Foots Cray. / *Tom Maddocks*

Below right: At the same spot but on a bright September day, revamped RF144 carries few passengers on Green Line route 719, whose half from London on the Kent side has since been incorporated into a new peak hour route, 729; at other times Maidstone & District 919 provides coverage. / *Tom Maddocks*

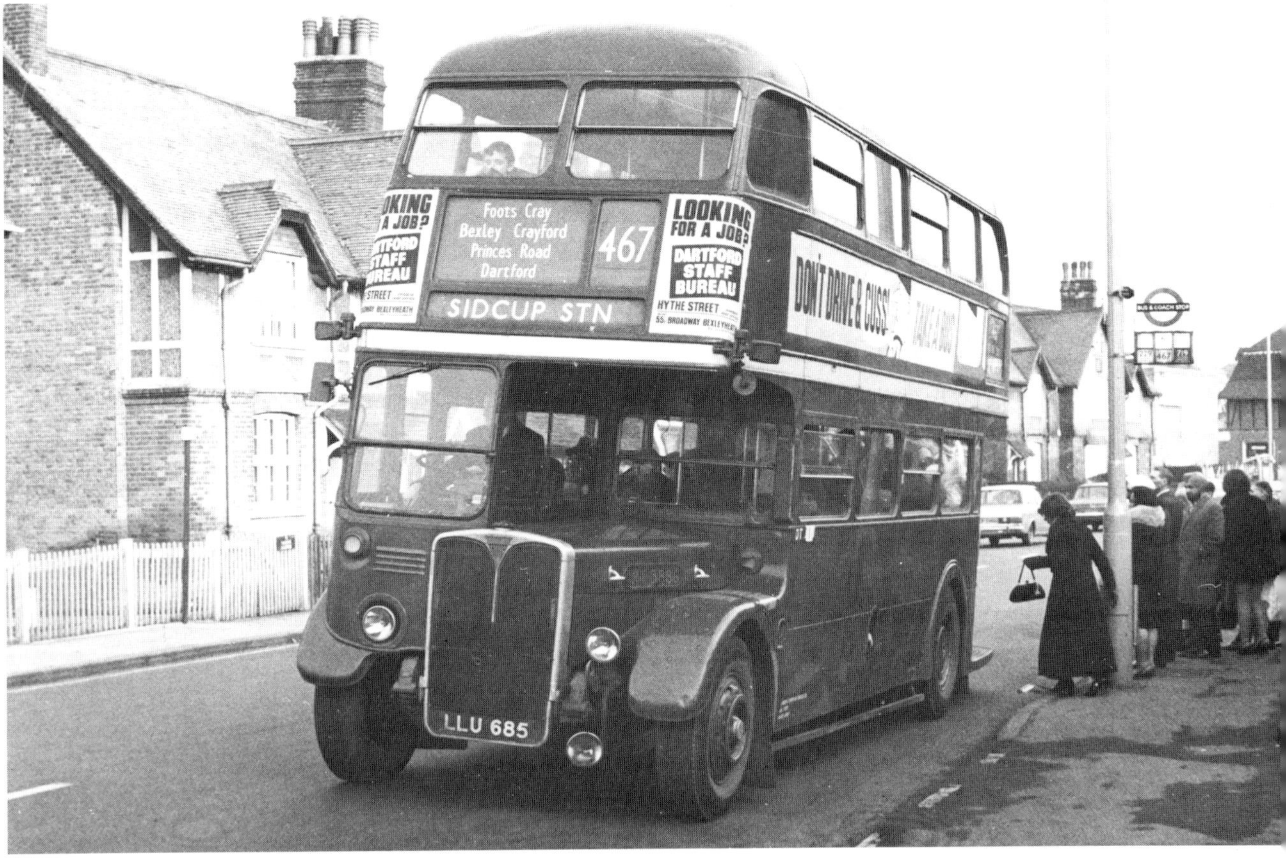
LOOKING FOR A JOB?
DARTFORD STAFF BUREAU
HYTHE STREET
55 BROADWAY BEXLEYHEATH
Foots Cray
Bexley Crayford
Princes Road
Dartford
467
SIDCUP STN
DON'T DRIVE & CUSS!
TAKE A BUS
LLU 685

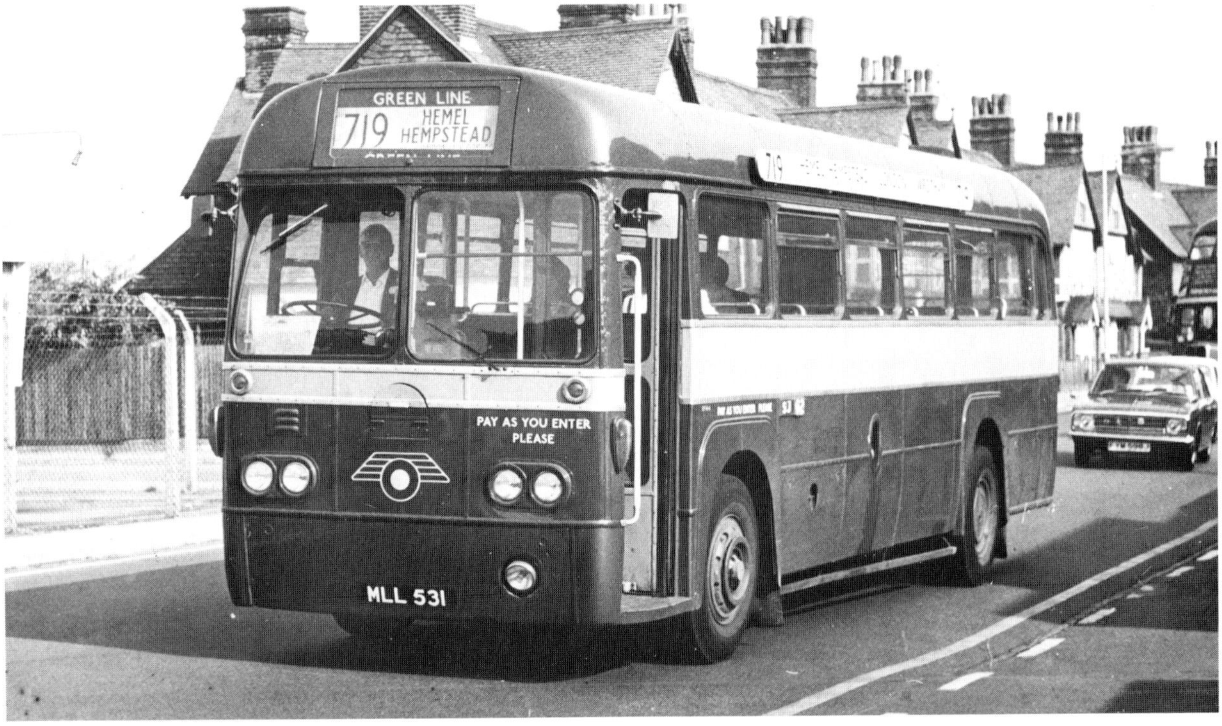
GREEN LINE
719 HEMEL HEMPSTEAD
PAY AS YOU ENTER
PLEASE
MLL 531

The Near South-East

Above: September 1971 at Bromley North station, terminus for Country routes 402 and 410 for very many years. Though RF582's paintwork is beginning to show signs of age, the bus was to last another four years before despatch for scrap. / *Tom Maddocks*

Left: The stop flag conveniently links the two routes. Some low-bridge STLs, of which STL2186 here at Bromley North station in 1952 was one, were transferred from Central Area to the Country Department, while ageing Country lowbridge STs from route 336 were moved simultaneously to Central Area duties. The wartime built bodies, on earlier regular STL chassis, had no rear indicators. / *D. W. K. Jones*

Above right: An inspector watches long Routemaster RML2325 move out from Bromley terminus for a departure on the 410 short journey to Biggin Hill as red Merlin MB319 terminates on route 126 during May 1972. / *Tom Maddocks*

Right: London Country's Daimler Fleetlines came new to Godstone garage for the 410 early in 1972. They operate as one-man crew buses. While red brother London Transport acquired well over 2,500 Fleetlines, London Country bought a mere 11, opting instead for the Leyland Atlantean as the regular rear-engined double-deck bus. The 11 have straightforward-looking bodywork by Northern Counties, fitted with dual doorways and liveried when new in 'light' — strictly a medium shade — National green and yellow. / *Tom Maddocks*

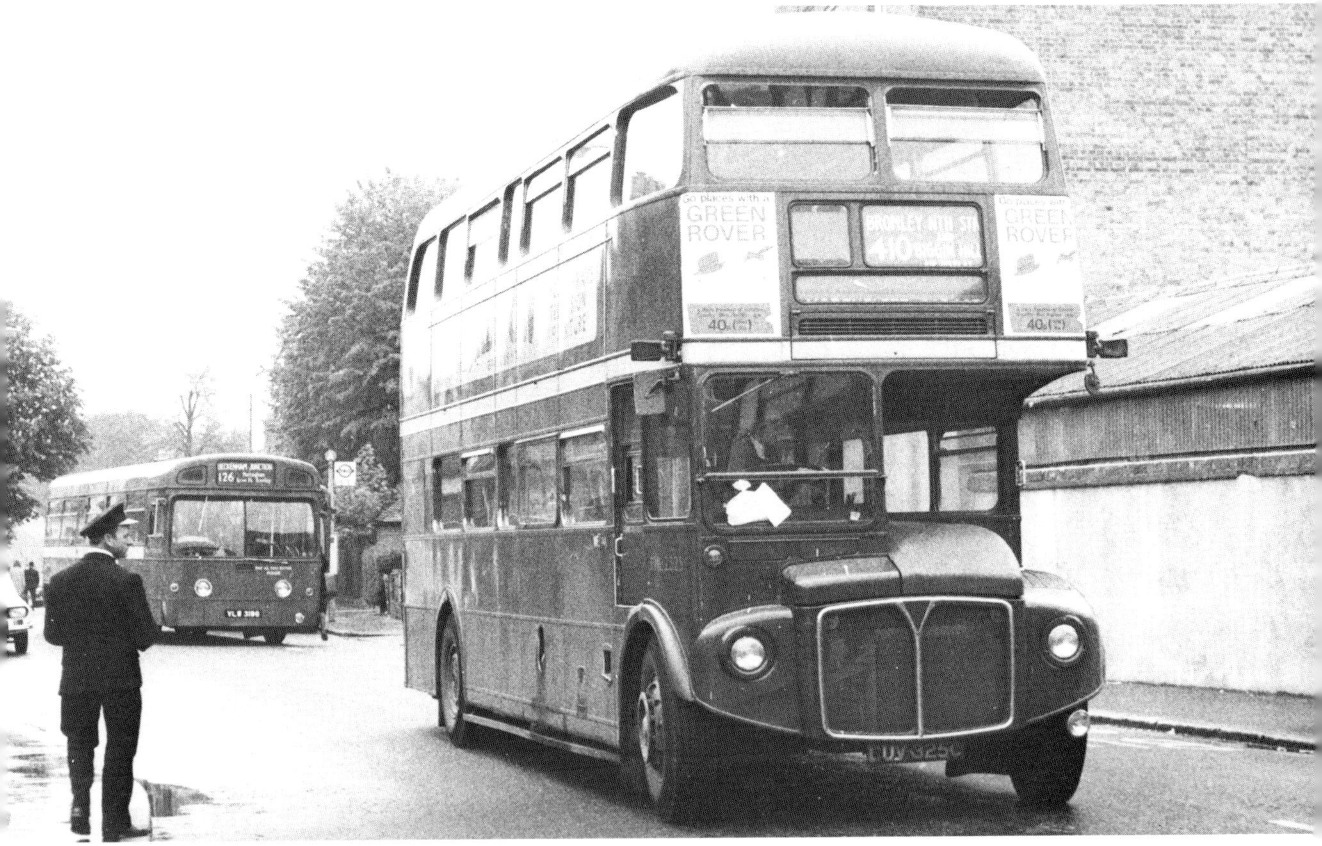
Go places with a
GREEN
ROVER
410
126

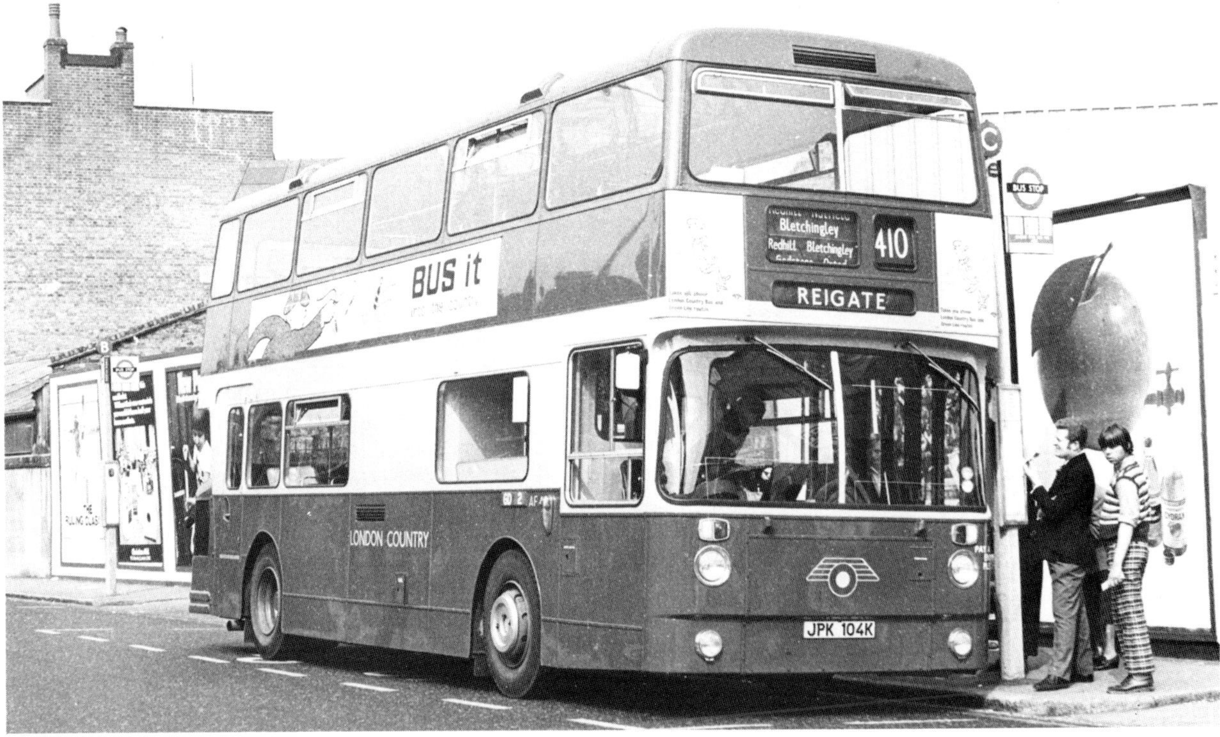
Bletchingley
Redhill Bletchingley
410
REIGATE
BUS it
LONDON COUNTRY
JPK 104K
BUS STOP

Above: Sometime operator of an 853 route to Croydon was North Downs Rural Transport, whose Strachans-bodied 16-seat Ford Transit stands at the Orpington terminus. / *John Fielder*

Right: Orpington station and a woman driver takes former coach RMC1478 on a 477 short journey, the six-minute run to Goddington Lane, in 1973. / *Edward Shirras*

West Kent

Left: In March 1967, Routemaster coaches were in the middle of their roundly 10-year term on front line Green Line work. With window beading painted in the intended relief colour, RMC1483 stands at Wrotham on the since discontinued route 717 to Welwyn Garden City. / *C. Carter*

Below: The temporary waiting room at Sevenoaks bus station was the ultimate task for London Six LS1, still in red livery after withdrawal from the Central Area in 1937. / *D. W. K. Jones*

Right: Route 401 from Belvedere no longer reaches as far south as Sevenoaks, where RT2874 was photographed passing solid urban architecture in St John's Hill in October 1968. / *C. Carter*

Below: Edenbridge in June 1957 and a little Guy, GS8, runs by gently on its way to Westerham. / *C. Carter*

Bottom: LNC39 came new to London Country in 1973 as a 'coach', though it could hardly justify that description from its appearance or its rather basic bus seating. This Tring garage vehicle stands at the summer extension terminus of route 706 at Chartwell. Of the 47 Leyland Nationals of this single doorway, 37ft 3in length type, some were used as buses from the outset, and the Green Line ones were so used later on. / *Edward Shirras*

West Sussex

Above: Sussex has always been a fringe area for London's green buses, but many route miles are worked in the county. Daimler Fleetlines were new to the Country Department when XF1 appeared on route 424 from East Grinstead in 1965. Later the class of eight went to the Central Area for comparative trials with Atlanteans, but then returned to the Country Area to be taken into LCBS stock on formation of the company. At the time of writing they still appear on some routes from their original home garage. / *D. W. K. Jones*

Left: The last three 'experimental' Fleetlines were painted blue and silver for a couple of years at the start of the 1970s for use on Stevenage's Blue Arrow service. XF7 should feel more at home back in its original East Grinstead haunts. Its livery is green again, now the National shade with white band. Reversion to capital letters for places mentioned on the route blind is interesting, after many years use of lower case lettering, reckoned easier to read. / *John A. Gray*

428 DORMANSLAND
LONDON COUNTRY
VPB 121M

409
DORMANSLAND
Make your outing
a national holiday
Day trips with
NATIONAL
LONDON COUNTRY
BUS & COACH STOP
6949 CD

Left: In May 1974, three Park Royal-bodied Atlanteans replaced three early 'experimental' Atlanteans from the XA type sold in the Far East a year previously. They were the first LCBS new double-deck buses to have three track number blinds and alongside one line indicators at the front. Here the first of the trio, AN121, traverses the new roundabout near East Grinstead railway station in November 1978. / *John A. Gray*

Below left: Another trio to work in the East Grinstead area was bought secondhand from Southdown Motor Services. They were Leyland Titan PD3s with Northern Counties front entrance bodywork, and they kept Southdown's rich green and yellowish cream livery for their short LCBS life. There's a welcome here for two ladies from someone aboard LS1. / *LCBS*

Above right: London Transport's T class just failed numerically to reach 800. The last duties for the final survivors of the T type, the fine Mann Egerton-bodied version classified as 15T13, were from Crawley garage, where T787 is shown with GS12 in 1960. / *D. W. K. Jones*

Centre right: Crawley garage yard is generally full of buses at weekends, and this September Sunday in 1971 was no exception. Today's buses would no longer be elderly RTs but Atlanteans bearing the 'C Line' logo of Crawley town services. / *D. W. K. Jones*

Below: London Country took over 15 Swifts from South Wales Transport in the summer of 1971. This posed view of SMW2, one of three with Willowbrook 60-passenger capacity (48 seated) bodywork, the heaviest on LC Swifts, shows how they looked when acquired. The bus was about two years old at the time. The three, with their dual doorways, have regularly run in the Crawley area, while the other 12 have worked from St Albans. / *LCBS*

473
EAST GRINSTEAD
434
LONDON COUNTRY
FIELDALE
Audi
UPB 327S

GO OUR WAY-WE'RE GOING YOURS
NATIONAL EXPRESS
C LINE
LONDON COUNTRY
UPK 142S
C2
LANGLEY GREEN

Above left: It's just after half-past two on a late autumn 1978 afternoon and there's a choice of two departures for East Grinstead. Leyland National SNB327 on route 434 will take the longer route through Copthorne and Crawley Down; the Merlin behind on the 473 should arrive earlier by taking a more direct route through Rowfant. / *John A. Gray*

Left: Crawley town routes were reorganised into a new system, called 'C Line', on 1 July 1978. Here, AN142 on route C7 waits in the bus station for departure to one of the neighbourhood areas as another C Line Atlantean comes in. / *John A. Gray*

Above: C Line Atlanteans and a Reliance/Plaxton coach line up at Crawley bus station one November afternoon in 1978. AN134 waits to start a journey on the irregular 438 route — not a C Line service and originated by Sargents of East Grinstead — while sister AN151 fills the gap next to RS35 bound for Luton Airport on the long 727 Green Line western orbital route. / *John A. Gray*

Centre right: The driver of this third batch Park Royal-bodied Atlantean glances in his mirror and an incognito passenger looks back as a forward view is captured of this newest variant, as at November 1978, of bodywork fitted to London Country's Atlanteans. It's a single-doorway version, and the 74 seats have a brownish yellow covering. / *John A. Gray*

Right: Early closing day at Langley Green shopping parade as AN139 arrives from Crawley bus station on C Line route C4. Blinds would be changed to C1 Rutherford Way before departure from this quiet neighbourhood centre. / *John A. Gray*

Above: One of the oldest service vehicles, dating from 1963, was in use for tree pruning towards the end of 1978 at Crawley bus station. 1241F is based on a Thames Trader lorry. The 'Thames' and 'Fordson' names were later discontinued by the Ford Motor Company. / *John A. Gray*

Right: Thirty years old and still teaching them to drive! RT981 winks right in Crawley. This bus was one of four given a light overhaul 18 months before this autumn 1978 picture, though it remained in the old Lincoln green livery. / *John A. Gray*

Above: Despite its being a circular route, the 426 has two termini in Crawley, at *The George* and the bus station. The first of the Alexander-bodied Swifts, SMA1, pulls in to the bus station in November 1978. The vehicle still wears National's Green Line livery. / *John A. Gray*

Centre left: The southern terminus of route 414 from Croydon to Horsham, where RT3202 was pictured leaving the railway station while working the route in June 1967. / *C. Carter*

Below left: The 414 was usually associated with double-deck buses, particularly RTs, for a long postwar period, but single-deck omo working had been introduced on Sundays by May 1970, when former Green Line RF42, in bus livery with all London Transport reference painted out, was photographed on the route at the Horsham end. The bus eventually went for scrap five years later. / *C. Carter*

Right: When still quite new, RF675 worked the lengthy 434 route running peripherally round a large segment of the southern area from Edenbridge to Horsham before the Crawley to Horsham portion was taken over by the 405 from Croydon in 1957 (though many years later the 434 was to regain Horsham). Here the bus pulls up at a public house whose sign post carries the bus stop flag, completing the period setting of the early 1950s. / *Don Morris*

Below: East Grinstead's small bus station had only MBS416 waiting to leave for its 70 minute journey via Turner's Hill, Crawley and Faygate to Horsham in this November 1978 picture. All London Country's Merlins have two door bodywork. This one is in the second Metro-Cammell bodied batch, seating only 33 passengers but with room for another 27 standing. / *John A. Gray*

East Surrey and Croydon

Left: Operated in turn by Autocar, East Surrey, London General Country Services and LPTB, ST1139, the last ST numerically, was the original AEC Regent demonstration vehicle. Here it draws away from the stop at Blindley Heath in September 1938 when working on route 409 from East Grinstead garage. / *D. W. K. Jones*

Below: Picture Post's well remembered eyes stare at the photographer. STL2417 in early wartime finish, with blanked out indicators, white wing tips and headlamp masks, stands outside Godstone garage sometime in 1940 as a fuel tanker makes a delivery. / *D. W. K. Jones*

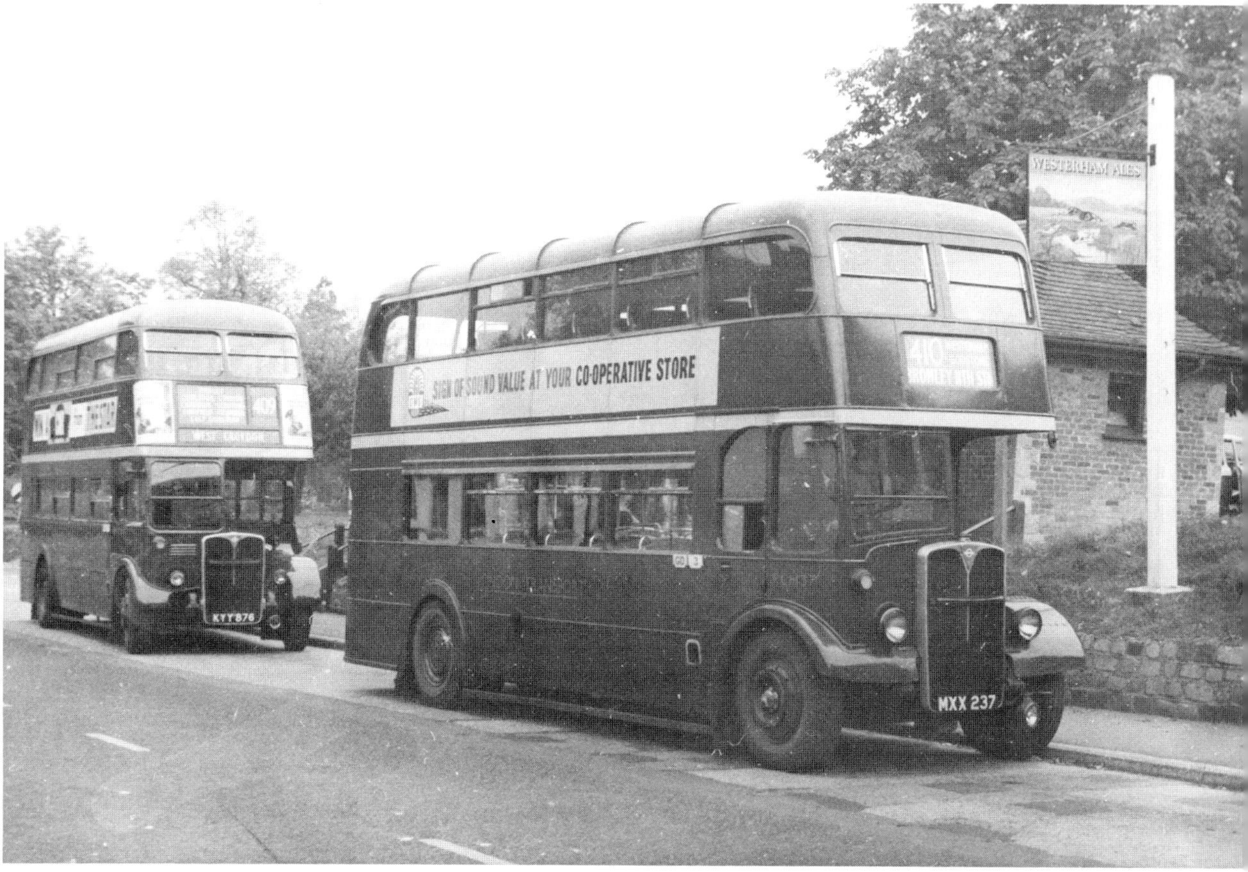
WESTERHAM ALES
SIGN OF SOUND VALUE AT YOUR CO-OPERATIVE STORE
410
KYY 876
MXX 237

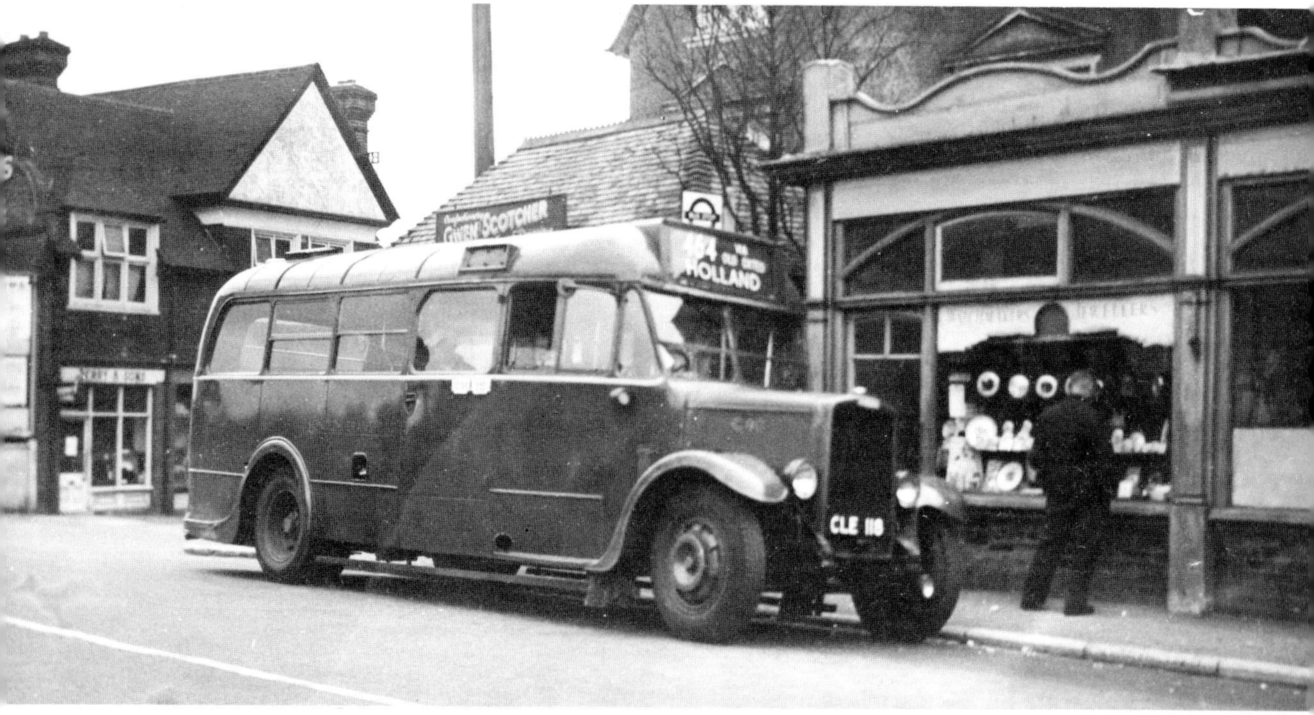
HOLLAND
CLE 118

Left: In October 1958, STLs had long since gone from route 409 and RTs had worked it for several years, as RT3147, here behind RLH37, on the 410 at Godstone. The photograph allows comparison between London and provincial bodywork styles dating from the immediate prewar period, as refined postwar, and built on closely alike AEC Regent chassis. / *C. Carter*

Below left: Oxted in the early 1950s, when Leyland Cubs with their distinctive sounds still worked route 464. C90 was built with Central Area operation in mind, and so was provided with an offside route number stencil holder in the roof side above the emergency exit but had no front bumper. / *Don Morris*

Above: The same spot not so very long afterwards found the Cubs' direct replacement, the Guy Specials, in the Oxted area. GS59 looks very new as it prepares to leave foı East Grinstead on the now withdrawn route 494. / *C. Carter*

Centre right: One that got away. While on the subject of that very rural route 494, let's look at a rare picture of an unlikely bus that was used on it at the end of its modest working life in the early 1950s. CR14 was one of 49 Leyland Cubs built in 1939-40, well after the standard Cubs, with one major difference from their name-counterparts: their engine was at the back, hence the complete absence of frontal radiator and bonnet, etc. It has been construed that the design inspiration so tried eventually materialised in the bulk production Atlantean.

Based on East Grinstead garage, CR14 was one of a handful of the type to have had a quick livery change to Lincoln green with white for what was presumed to be its final year. However, this bus got away in another sense: it avoided the scrap merchant by being bought for preservation, and at the time of writing, CR14 still exists, back in red livery. / *D. W. K. Jones*

Below right: Chelsham yard in 1953 and brand new Guy GS7 stands superior to a row of its predecessors. Leyland Cubs C61, C4 and C59 are identifiable reading from left. / *D. W. K. Jones*

Above: Chelsham garage 19 years on, October 1972, has on show the London Country 'winged wheel' device angled proudly above a pair of AEC Regal IVs. RF177, nearer, was a modernised Green Line coach, by now on bus work, and RF640, always a bus, shows that by then buses bigger than Cubs could work the 464's changed routeing. / *C. Carter*

Centre left: Gordon's Maudslay, as it was affectionately known to many London enthusiasts of the era, found less favour with LPTB operating staff. This Maudslay ML7 had a Dodson body and was new in 1931. Numbered 7 in the small Gordon fleet, it had worked route 511, Stratford-Chingford. Shorn of its sun roof, interior clock and other luxury appointments, it ended its days on the 408 from Leatherhead garage. It was allocated the fleet number MY1. The other 12 Maudslays acquired by the Board didn't last to receive fleet numbers. ST1139 on route 405 draws up close behind at Croydon. / *D. W. K. Jones*

Below left: Long Routemaster 'coach' RCL2244 would have given a comfortable ride on this route 414 departure from West Croydon bus station to Horsham in March 1974. Interestingly, the bus carries the LCBS motif on the staircase side panel, while the side length poster displays the NBC emblem. / *C. Carter*

Above right: Moving out from the bus station at Croydon in April 1977 is RT1018, the first of the dwindled RT type to receive National Bus corporate livery. / *C. Carter*

Right: In October 1975, MBS4 took a turn from West Croydon on the 414. This last remnant of London Transport's original experimental Strachan's-bodied standee Merlins is the only one to have been overhauled. / *C. Carter*

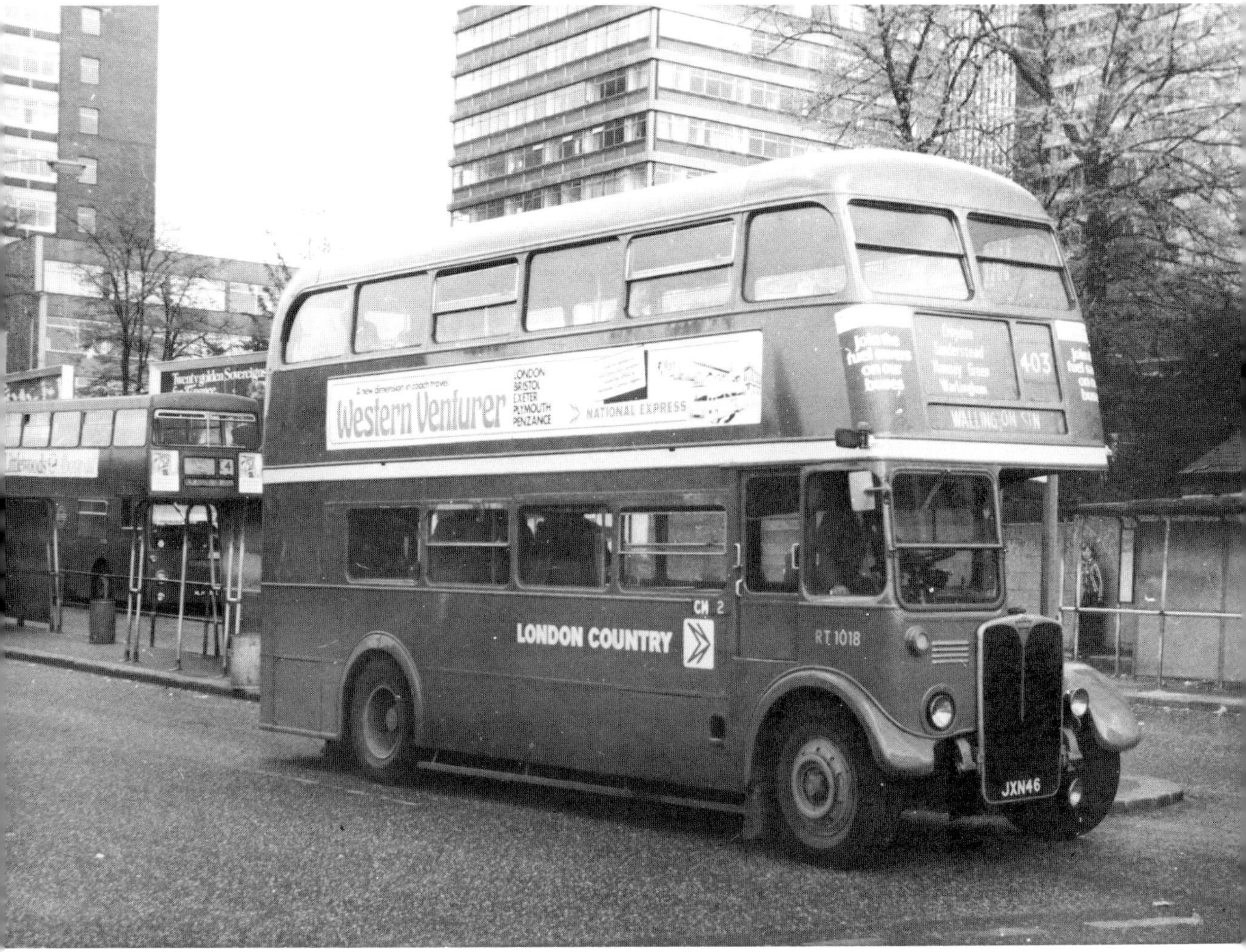

Twenty golden Sovereigns
A new dimension in coach travel
Western Venturer
LONDON
BRISTOL
EXETER
PLYMOUTH
PENZANCE
NATIONAL EXPRESS
403
WALLINGTON STN
CM 2
LONDON COUNTRY
RT 1018
JXN46

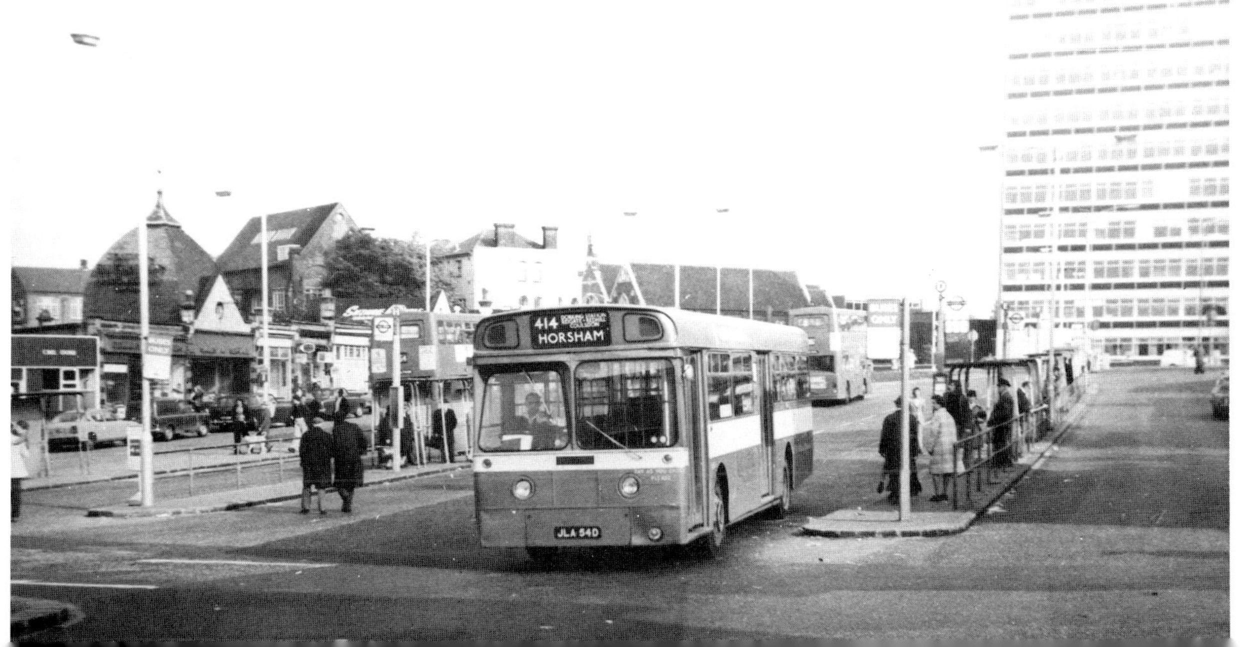

414
HORSHAM
JLA 54D

Redhill and Reigate

Left: Britain's major railways combined to compete against *inter alia* bus travel in the transport market in this *circa* 1934 picture of ST1097B inside Reigate garage. The fleet number suffix letters B, C were presumed to distinguish suitability for either bus work or coach duty. The 406 still runs to much the same Kingston-Redhill route. / *H. J. Snook*

Below: Route 406 in August 1971 finds RT4497 bound for Redhill. Operating out of Leatherhead garage, the bus has lost its green AEC radiator badge but retains its rear wheel hub covers. / *Tom Maddocks*

Top: Reigate garage from time to time held some interesting vehicles in store. These early Leyland Titans, stored in 1937, show great variety: left to right — ex-Maidstone & District highbridge TD159; ex-M&D former open top TD147; ex-Aston TD172; ex-M&D lowbridge TD153, and ex-Thames Valley TD168. */ D. W. K. Jones*

Above: The original Central Area Q1, side-engined AEC Q model dating from 1932, was afterwards transferred to the Country Department and became Q1B. Here it was working the one-time Redhill area route 460 in 1937. There were no outside running number plate slots, so the stencils were posted inside. */ D. W. K. Jones*

410
KESTON
BROMLEY NTH STN
LONDON TRANSPORT
BXD 546

410
BROMLEY NORTH STN
LONDON TRANSPORT
STL 1054
BPF 457

Above left: Single-deckers were always rare on the 410, for so long the preserve of lowbridge STLs, but Q25 worked Reigate-Redhill-Bromley in summer 1948. / *D. W. K. Jones*

Left: Lowbridge STL1054 was one of the 12 distinctive Weymann-bodied buses known as the 'Godstone STLs' as they spent nearly their whole lives working the well-known southern radial route 410 out of Godstone garage. Here it is at Hardwicke Road, Reigate. / *D. W. K. Jones*

Above: A few weeks after its September 1978 delivery, Atlantean AN180 leans a little on Reigate garage's sloping forecourt. Interesting use of the former LCBS symbol outline has been made to accommodate the reflected N symbol on the pole through the enquiry office verandah. / *John A. Gray*

Centre right: Green Lines at Reigate: this posed but nonetheless delightful period study from about 1934 of AEC Regal T220 well repays a close look at the clear details, right down to the lightened sidewall tyres! / *H. J. Snook*

Right: In 1965, London Transport took delivery of its longest vehicles up till then. They were 14 AEC Reliances with 49-seat Willowbrook coachwork finished in a new livery of pastel grey with a Lincoln green waistband. This particular version was not perpetuated, and after a chequered career some, as RC11 here in August 1971, were used on Green Line route 711 from Reigate, but in the standard Lincoln and pale greens. / *Tom Maddocks*

Left: Plaxton-bodied RS36 changes drivers at Bell Street in November 1978. New six months earlier, the coach shows signs of slight damage at the front nearside. Such adorned coachwork cannot make for straightforward repair. / *John A. Gray*

Below: Over to contemporary Redhill for Phase Two Leyland National SNB326 arriving at the Market Hall stop on the service introduced after withdrawal of Green Line route 711. The bus displays precious little information about its northbound journey. / *John A. Gray*

Right: A winter 1972 shot of Daimler Fleetline XF3 as it nears Reigate after a journey on the long-established twisty route 424. / *C. Carter*

Below right: This Bristol LS5G registered PHW918, like most other demonstrators, was based for a while on Reigate garage. The photograph was taken at the *Red Lion*, Reigate, in 1953, a time when route 447 still ran out to Woldingham. This 'lightweight' bus had a Gardner engine and Eastern Coach Works 45-seat body finished in an approximation to Lincoln green with polished aluminium lining and Green Line fleetnames. London Transport remained faithful to the AEC family. / *D. W. K. Jones*

BEA Croydon Travel Centre
GREEN ROVER
424
REIGATE
GREEN ROVER
CUV 53C

WOLDINGHAM
REDHILL
MERSTHAM
CATERHAM
447
Bristol
GREEN LINE
GREEN LINE
PHW 918

Above: Back to the Reigate headquarters vicinity. Looking as though it had been there for a long time, CR34, a Central Area rear-engined Cub, stands stored in the garage in May 1952. / *D. W. K. Jones*

Below: Standing proud on the garage forecourt, RF278 displays the earlier National livery. Despite this effort, the bus was withdrawn and disposed of early in 1976. The abbreviated front indicator allows a shortened message. / *LCBS*

Above: Frontal comparisons between 72-seaters: Leyland engined Daimler Fleetline CRL6-30 AF2 with Northern Counties body; and two Atlanteans model PDR1A/1Spl. AN78's bodywork is by Park Royal; AN120's by Metro-Cammell. / *LCBS*

Below: London Transport's red Swifts SMD62 and SMD94 stand on the forecourt one Saturday in November 1978, taking a rest from duties on staff transport. / *John A. Gray*

Above right: A disapproving glance from the man at the back as RT3752's driver emerges. By November 1978, this 24-year old RT, after a spell as a Windsor staff bus — hence WR code — was relegated further to a trainer. Its livery is light green and yellow, and it keeps its obsolete original London Country motif. / *John A. Gray*

Centre right: Secondhand Reliance RN1 with Plaxtons' Panorama Elite 60-seat coachwork was more familiar with the Nottingham area than with Reigate. Barton Transport was the first owner.

The back view of the Leyland National shows London Country's principle of having the rear route display panelled over, unlike red sisters in central London, where at least provision is made for the route number to be shown, / *John A. Gray*

Below: Bell Street fills the view beyond SNB357 as it turns out from Lesbourne Road in thin November sunshine, 1978. The old East Surrey buildings are on the right. / *John A. Gray*

Green in Red

Above: Green Line routes have always penetrated the heart of the red bus area, though since London Country's inception, fewer of them cross from one side to the other.

Still in the earliest and dignified olive green and black livery of Green Line Coaches is Regal T251, in 1935, at the Eccleston Bridge concentration of Green Line operation, Victoria. / *D. W. K. Jones*

Below: Enthusiasts today might give a lot to ride in this Leyland Titan — yes; it's not a Tiger — to Sevenoaks. Naturally numbered in the Titan series, TD175 came from Premier Line Ltd, about the only operator of single-deck Titans in London's express services. This example came to LPTB with 18 other Titan coaches from Premier Line, and they served their new owner well for several years. / *D. W. K. Jones*

Left: Another example of a bus relieving a Green Line coach route was Cravens-bodied RT1517, here in all Lincoln green livery apart from a cream band, having lost its cream surrounds to the upper windows and black wings.

Below: Back to the numerically largest single-deck T class Regals and to T354C in particular. This was one of a rebodied group whose later role was more usually that of a green or red bus rather than as here, a Green Line 'coach'. T354C had started life as a Harrington-bodied coach of Queen Line coaches on a London-Hitchin-Baldock service. After a period with Green Line on the same duties, this and other Queen Line and BlueBelle coaches with non-standard coachwork were rebodied for LT by MCW, and consequently saw many years of service. Here at Golders Green in May 1936 (showing a little of the still extant variety theatre), T354C worked route T, the Watford to Golders Green tube railway feeder. / *D. W. K. Jones*

Right: Finally to the best-remembered Green Line Regal type, classified 10T10 by LT. The wartime revival of the prewar lettered Green Line routes in summer 1940 saw T714 in remarkably good condition at Portman Square on route N to Bishop's Stortford. Wartime blackout restrictions dictated almost obscuring the driving lamps. / *D. W. K. Jones*

Below right: Kings Cross coach station, though a busy terminus for many concerns, never became the household name as London Coastal Coaches' Victoria did. It remained little used by Green Line, except for Luton routes.

Here in about 1949 is TF43, one of the Leyland Tiger FEC models to pioneer the underfloor engine concept, on route 727. This route did not cross London (though it was later part of a link to Dorking) and so was more in line with today's trend to have radial routes terminating centrally.

BISHOP'S STORTFORD
GREEN LINE N1
N
CAMDEN TOWN FINSBURY PARK
MANOR HOUSE TOTTENHAM HALE
WALTHAMSTOW WOODFORD
BUCKHURST HILL LOUGHTON
EPPING FOREST EPPING
EYK 349

727 LONDON LUTON 727
LS 55
TF 43
GREEN LINE
FJJ 654

Right: The highly secret coach, RTC1, reflects so much it would do well itself advertising a wonder polish. Rebuilt in the late 1940s from prewar design RT97, this Chiswick product was surrounded by so much secrecy during its creation that it almost became a legend before its release into service, first into Green Line work, as here on the 715, and later on Country bus work from Leatherhead garage. During its quiet decline into obscurity in the early 1950s possibly some lessons were drawn for the then embryo designs for the Routemaster. / *S. A. Newman*

Below: The Routemaster, arguably the most comfortable double-decker produced in Britain, in its shorter length coach form. RMC1512 traverses Hyde Park Corner in July 1971 in style, without posters and with London Country's new insignia.
/ *Tom Maddocks*

Above: One of the Reliances with Park Royal bodywork heads out of the centre of Richmond along Petersham Road in October 1975 on route 716 to Chertsey. Unlike this member, the first 30 RPs had a luggage boot at the rear. / *John A. Gray*

Centre right: This Dennis Arrow coach, one of four to come from Red Rover Coaches' London-Aylesbury service, was numbered DL38 and used mainly for private hire. At Wembley Empire Pool/Stadium in 1936 on hire to Dean & Dawson, it carries the dual Green Line and London Transport fleetnames usual at the time for private hire coaches. / *D. W. K. Jones*

Right: Of 23 Thornycrofts acquired by the Board, the majority came from People's Motor Services of Ware, and this was one of the few reasonably modern ones. However, its youth did not save it, and by May 1936 it was sold out of service. Here it awaited a buyer, in Clapham Road. / *D. W. K. Jones*

Country Life Ended

Above: A vehicle whose country life ended almost as soon as it had begun was this one. Registered UR4642, it was one of the more spectacular buses used by the small operators in and around St Albans: a long, low Daimler CF6, operated by Flower & Etches. It had an 'all weather' canvas roof, and was painted light blue with a broad light band exaggerating its length. In 1934 it was operated briefly by the Board before being sold. / *D. W. K. Jones*

Below: Unloved Dennis 30cwt registered GU7544, one of two vehicles contributed by A. Howes, was distinguishable by its odd diamond-shaped side windows at the rear. It had worked from Amersham garage late in 1935. / *D. W. K. Jones*

Above: GMC 'Sun Saloon' was the epithet of this small canvas roofed coach. It was one of the more unlikely vehicles to be inherited by the Country Department from LGCS. It had reached a breaker's crammed yard in Brixton by October 1936.
/ D. W. K. Jones

Below: Whoops! Country STL524's bodywork parts company with the chassis in a Suffolk breakers yard to give a very tall effect.
/ Don Morris

Red Connections: South-West

Above: Morden station approach was very crowded at the time of this summer 1933 photograph when Country Department ST833, by now graced with the General fleetname, was loading for a journey to Dorking on route 70D. Very unusually, operation of the route was shared between the Central and Country bus departments for some years through the 1930s. Red STL400 is the other AEC Regent. / *John Fielder*

Right: The Great Western Railway's advertisement on ST1055 dates this picture to 1936, in the summer, judging by the open windows. For a couple of years now the D suffix had been dropped and the route was plain 70 to green as well as red buses. Successor route 470 remains much the same over the Sutton to Dorking length. / *John Fielder*

Above: One of Britain's bestknown racing occasions, Derby Day, brings out many vehicles to help move the crowds visiting Epsom Downs for the day's sport. ST189 leads an early postwar procession of similar buses on the special service from the Northern Line tube railhead at Morden. / *John Fielder*

Left: Open staircase former Tilling ST906 in red livery helps the Country Department by spending an early postwar Derby Day on the special 406F route that links Epsom station with the Downs. / *A. M. Wright*

EPSOM
305
DGX 383

EPSOM STATION
406F AND
EPSOM DOWNS
RMC1459
459 CLT
MAC'S
...and a box of please

Left: Prewar loudspeaker van, number 305M in the olive green service fleet, stands at the ready at Epsom station soon after the war. Based on the Morris-Commercial chassis, the vehicle looks as though it could have found later use as a minibus. / *Alan B. Cross*

Below left: By the 1970s Routemaster coaches and RTs take up duty on the 406F. Green Line liveried RMC1459 heads the rank comprising an RT, two bus RMCs, an ice cream van and another RT. / *LCBS*

Above: Over to Kingston-upon-Thames now, where SMA7 moves smartly across traffic lanes in Wood Street after stopping to allow red bus interchange with this Green Line journey on route 725 as far as Dartford in October 1977. / *John A. Gray*

Below: Green light for Green Line coach RB27 on route 726, picking its way through Kingston's dense Saturday traffic. This vehicle came in the first batch of 15 Reliances built with Duple Dominant II coachwork and had not long been delivered when photographed in autumn 1977. / *John A. Gray*

Above: Day tours were and are attractions offered by LT from time to time. One of the most popular postwar tours was to Hampton Court and Windsor. This LTC, a late-built three-axle AEC Renown, rests outside Cardinal Wolsey's palace at Hampton Court whilst its passengers tire themselves in the maze, perhaps. / *D. W. K. Jones*

Below: Kingston bus station, effectively the front portion of the garage, has always had a variety of interesting vehicles to show. Here in 1952, former Country buses Q21 and T469 rub shoulders on Central Area routes.

LT was seldom at a loss to use any spare wall space for advertising revenue. The smoking prohibition notice above Q21 rather conflicts with the nearby smokers' match advertisement! / *D. W. K. Jones*

Above right: Green and red routes both use Kingston railway station's forecourt as a terminal, diagonally across the road from the red routes only bus station. RT987, in its last six months of LCBS' life, collects girls for the Redhill ride while SM109 waits for departure time on route 418: July 1976. / *John A. Gray*

Right: Fifteen months later and RMC1471 works the 406 while ladies discuss the prospect of boarding RN1, the first of the 60-seater AEC Reliance dual-purpose vehicles acquired from Barton Transport, doing a stint on route 418. / *John A. Gray*

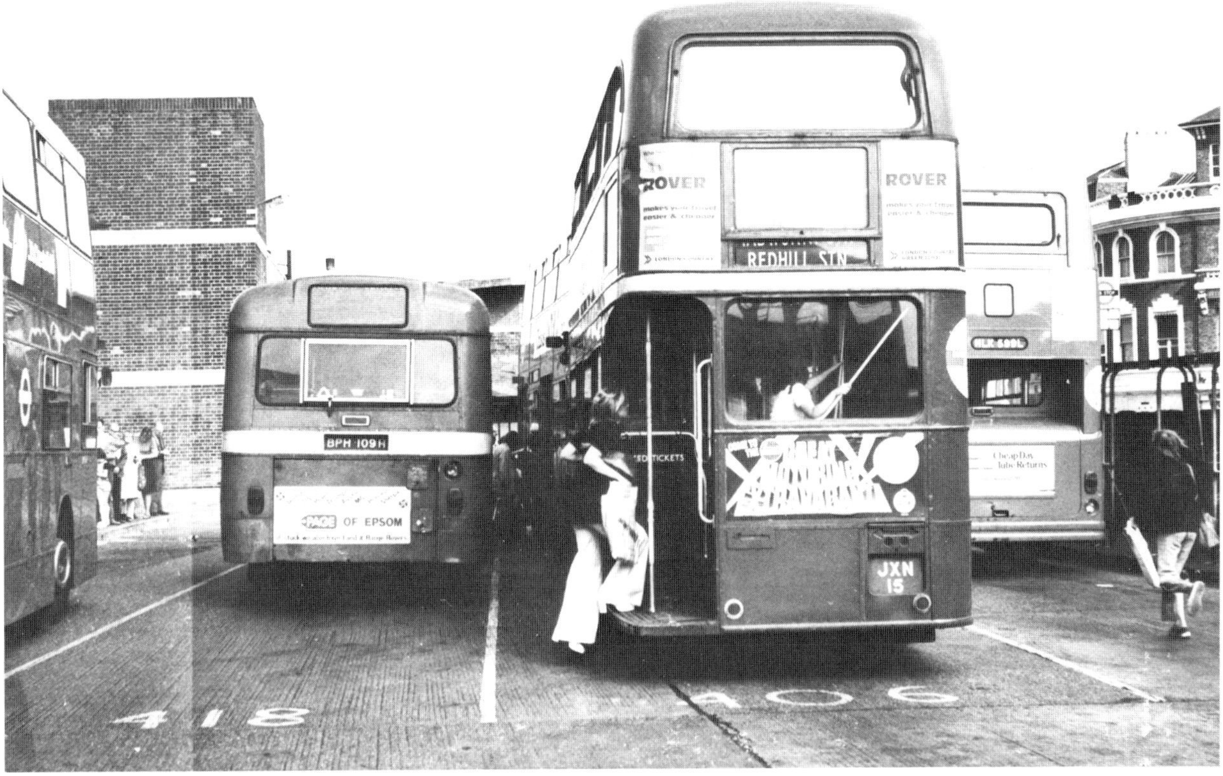
ROVER
ROVER
REDHILL STN
BPH 109H
OF EPSOM
JXN 15
Cheap Day Tube Returns
418
406

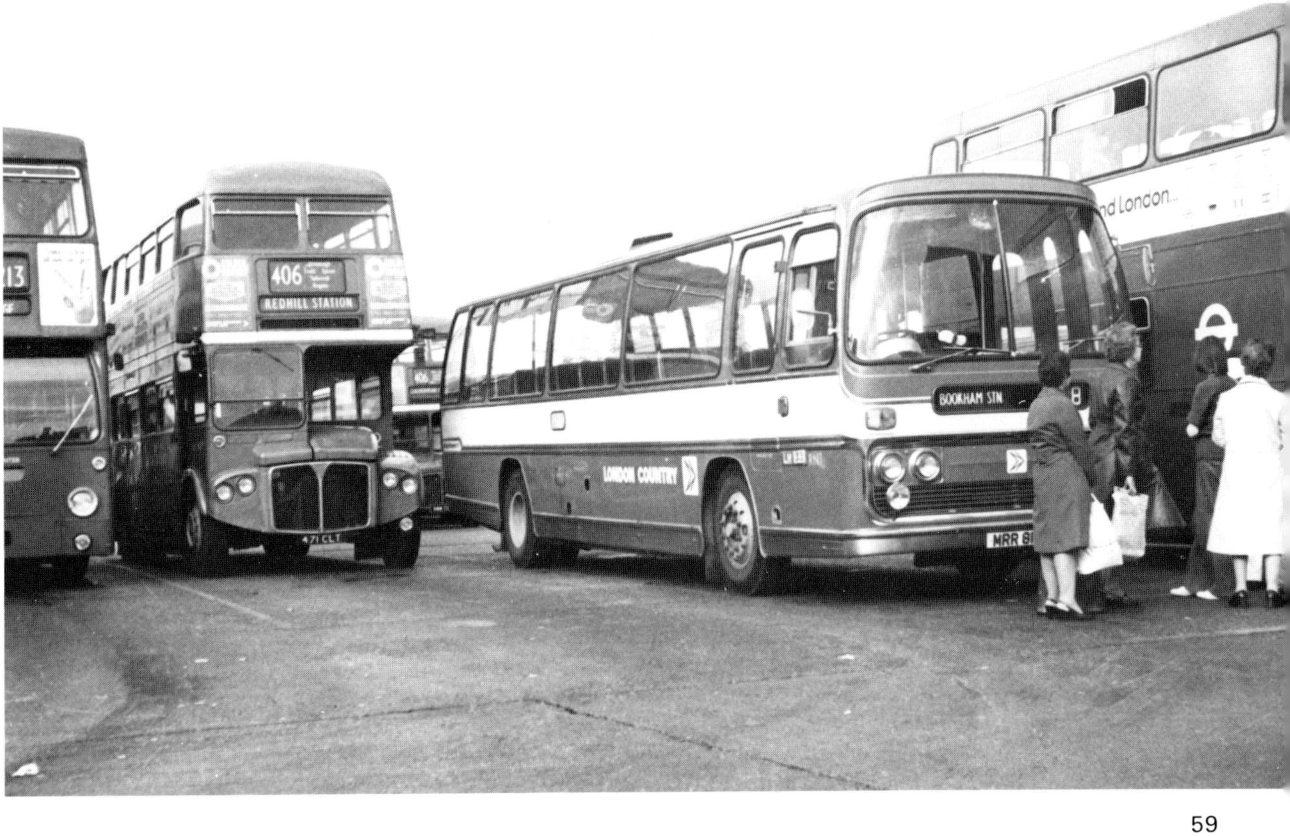
406
REDHILL STATION
471 CLT
BOOKHAM STN
LONDON COUNTRY

Western North Downs

Above: The village policeman plods in from the left of this sleepy scene at Leigh in May 1956. RT4161 ticks over at the fare stage on its strange part circular, part one-ended way by route 439 to Reigate and Redhill. Nearly 10 years later the route was to revert to single-deck operation. / *C. Carter*

Left: Ranmore had the services of route 433 until 1968 when the 412 took over. In this scene, Cub C45, complete with wartime white painted disc on the rear wall, waits by the unobtrusive and rusting miniature stop flag once used occasionally in country areas. The 433 worked through Dorking from Ranmore to Coldharbour, yet for some years during Cub operation, its bus (the route needed only one) worked out from Leatherhead garage. / *John Fielder*

Below left: For many years route 412 has had a terminus at Sutton — the green one, as evidenced here in October 1977. In a sense the narrow Bristol LHSs — it's BN44 shaded by the trees — are the modern counterpart of the Leyland Cubs in that they were designed for use over narrow roads. / *John A. Gray*

Left: Over the hill in the next valley, C95 rounds the bend to cross the culverted stream and pull into this picturesque stop on route 448 in returning to Guildford sometime in the late 1940s. / *John Fielder*

Below: Same route, 448, and perhaps the expected vehicle, GS3; but a different operator. Tillingbourne Valley Bus Services had taken over LT's responsibility for the route, and with it, some of the useful Guy Specials with their sturdy Eastern Coach Works' 26-seat bodywork, not so very long before this March 1965 scene at the top of Newlands Corner. / *D. W. K. Jones*

Top: Earlier days for Tillingbourne Valley: a March 1955 shot of a brown-liveried Bedford OB with Plaxton coachwork on the local Guildford route to Warren Road. / *C. Carter*

Above: Back to the earlier days at Guildford. Thrown out hastily by the Central Area after a short experience of their unreliability, these former independent-owned Dennis H-type double-deckers afflicted the Windsor area until early in 1936, when the Country Department withdrew the lot for scrapping. Awaiting their fate at the rear of Guildford garage in the March of that year are four from the Paterson Omnibus Company's fleet, one from Birch Bros and one from BBP Omnibus Co. The large-radiator version was in fact the HV model, but all were known as 'DH' to LT. / *D. W. K. Jones*

Western Thames-Side

Left: Walton-on-Thames Motor Company, sandwiched between London Transport's red and green bus areas, and, as though forgotten by the metropolitan monster and never taken over by it, continued to provide a town to station link service over many years. Eventually the service ceased, and was replaced within a few days in January 1970 by a Golden Miller route, later numbered 604. This Dennis Ace and a Bedford were in regular use in 1937. / *D. W. K. Jones*

Below: A 'Godstone' STL pays a visit to Walton-on-Thames on route 461A — which did not need lowbridge buses — in July 1952. STL1055 demonstrates well the sliding doors to the front entrance. The tween-decks cream band had consumed the original front destination line box! / *C. Carter*

Top: Thornycroft NY5 originally with Peoples, Ware, shows a blind for 456 to Woking station. LT concentrated most of the Thornycrofts it acquired at Weybridge (Addlestone), labelling them the NY type, irrespective of variations. Their size suited the twisting narrow roads of the Chertsey area, but they were less than popular with the crews. / *D. W. K. Jones*

Above: Addlestone garage in the early LCBS period of the early 1970s and two of the provincial type AEC Regent Mk IIIs with local Weymann lowbridge bodywork, RLHs 14 and 44, stand ready for the 461 road to Staines. / *C. Carter*

Top right: The same spot about seven years later; the buses have gone down a size but the garage chimney has been built up one! At a time when external maintenance standards on Swifts, Merlins and Routemasters weren't what they had been, WY garage displayed two smart Swifts. In front, SM118, in National green and white with red, white and blue symbol, stands ready for route 420, once a Byfleet-Woking local, but by now extended considerably at both ends. Behind, a sister with the first style National symbol waits to leave on the then new 459 route penetrating London Transport's area to Feltham. / *John A. Gray*

Centre right: Reliance RP55 on Green Line route 716 picks up in Addlestone for the journey to 'London, Oxford Circus' as SM107 draws up close behind on the long established 462 route to Leatherhead; July 1978. / *John A. Gray*

Right: A comparatively little-known class of just three vehicles was LT's RW type, introduced in 1960 for experiments in loading with a body having separate entrance and exit. They were LT's first Reliances, and the only ones with the small (by London standards) 7.7 litre engine. The Willowbrook bodywork seated 42, and was liveried in standard Lincoln green but with a cream band rather than having the window frame line in cream, as Country RFs. The RWs were tried under varying traffic conditions from Addlestone, Hemel Hempstead and Reigate garages before settling at St Albans, where they remained till sold to Chesterfield Corporation. This view of RW3 was taken in 1961, when all three were garaged at Addlestone. / *D. W. K. Jones*

RIPLEY
LONDON COUNTRY

716 LONDON
GREEN LINE
JPA155K

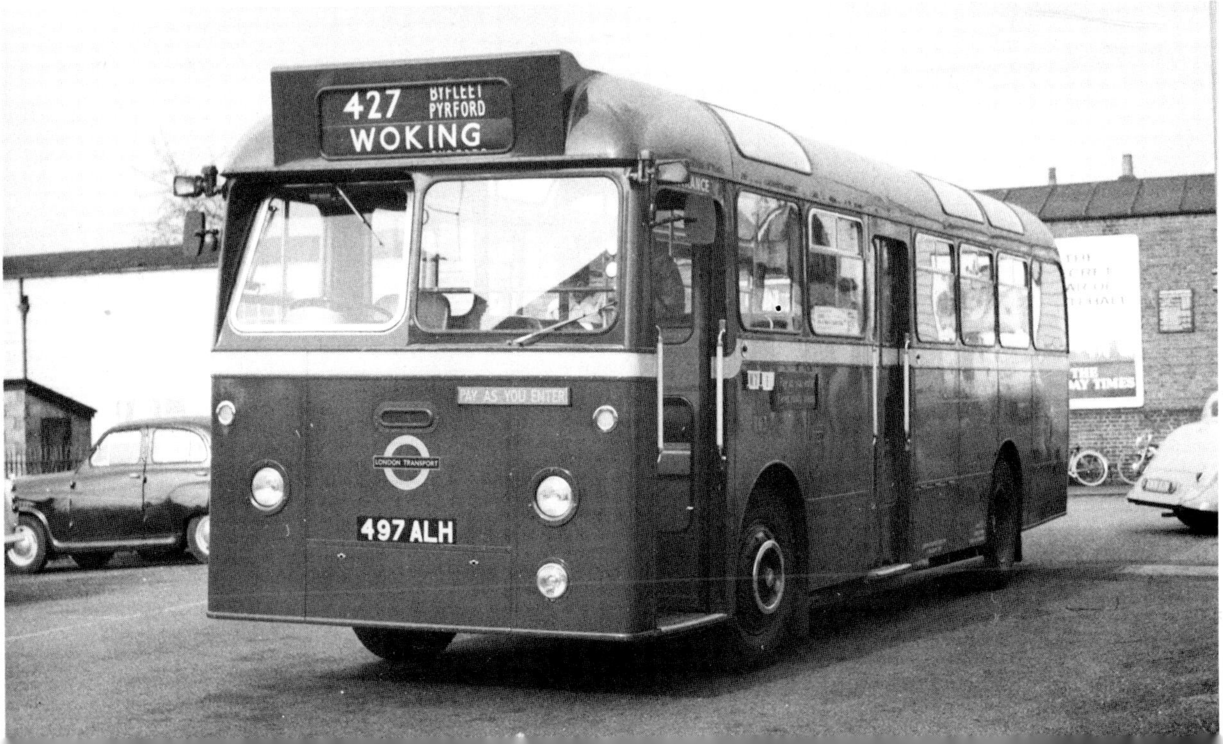

Above: In July 1978, SM131 doesn't yet feel quite at home in the thick of red buses at Feltham. The 'alighting point only' qualifier under a standard LT compulsory stop flag marks where route 459 terminates at Highfield Road. Feltham station, a few hundred yards further on, would seem to be a more natural terminus, were it not so congested. The 459, whose number was previously used for the postwar Uxbridge to Thorney (Richings Park) route, covers the former LT RF-operated outer section of route 237 to Chertsey, and is projected thence to Addlestone. The rear blind space used for advertising could receive plenty of glances. / *John A. Gray*

Below: Back to a riverside town; Staines; though many a photographers' favourite area is not by the Thames but outside the old West railway station, alongside a minor distributary of the River Colne. T442 was one of 50 coaches coded 9T9, entering service in 1936 with bodywork built by LPTB's Chiswick works to seat 30 people. After war service as ambulances and mobile canteens for troops, the survivors found their way to Country bus service, as here in 1949. / *D. W. K. Jones*

Above: Lowbridge ST140 had a Short Bros' 48-seat body incorporating top deck 'island' seating — forward facing rows of three seats placed centrally, with a gangway on either side against the windows. There were eight buses generally similar, and they outlived their majority counterparts by a couple of years till enough RLHs came. ST140 displays a blind for the rare 462C and still looks well even in its twilight years. / *S. A. Newman*

Left: The replacing type — still an AEC Regent, 20 years on — was the Weymann-bodied RLH. More of the flowing waters are apparent in this circa 1952 view of a still quite new RLH26. / *Don Morris*

Above: Trees can grow a lot in 24 years. RT4187 was a Country Department bus when new, but by the end of its life it was an LT red-liveried trainer. Keeping it company is one of Golden Miller's three Bedford YMTs with Plaxtons Derwent semi-standee bodywork. One bus is needed for the hourly route 606 journeys to Stanwell Village or Stanwellmoor. 'The Moor' as it's familiarly known was still served by London Country's route 444 on Saturdays in June 1976 when this picture was taken. / *John A. Gray*

Below: A gravelled area at the side of the only Country garage in former Middlesex, Staines, is used from time to time for buses out of use for longer periods. Two Country Department Qs with Birmingham Railway Carriage & Wagon Co bodywork stood there for this picture taken in about 1953. Scratched Q97 shows a Green Line Relief blind for 701 London/Ascot while Q72 behind shows only four tungsten lamp holders. / *Don Morris*

Above: Several Daimler Roadliners were borrowed from Bournemouth Corporation on a rota basis during the bus shortage in the 1970s. Stationed at Staines garage, the yellow rear-engined buses were often to be seen working on route 460, as here in Staines High Street, No 56, in June 1976. The low driving position is at a similar level to that in earlier Merlins. / *John A. Gray*

Below: The wrap-round rear windows of Bournemouth's No 60 give a lead to the bodybuilder — Willowbrook. Daimler Roadliners were fitted traditionally with the rather noisy Cummins engine. / *John A. Gray*

Above: The red livery of London General Country Services predominated in 1932-33, supplanting the red and off-white of East Surrey and the National Transport companies. Former East Surrey Regent registered APC162, later to become ST1032, and a similar bus stand at Windsor Castle in June 1933. / *D. W. K. Jones*

Below: In prewar days when keeping left wasn't quite the universal rule of Britain's roads it was to become, R43 stands on what would now be strictly the wrong side of the street, beneath the castle's curtain wall, waiting to leave on route 457 in 1936. Batten's Coaches, a substantial operator in east London, contributed this and many similarly pleasing AEC Reliances to the LT fleet. / *D. W. K. Jones*

Above right: Windsor Castle is the meeting point of Country and Thames Valley — now Alder Valley — services and those of a handful of independent operators. In the foreground is the Dennis Ace of White Bus Services which, uniquely, traversed Windsor Great Park via the Copper Horse statue. On its offside stands a Thames Valley Tilling-Stevens destined for South Ascot, and an ST comes up Thames Street, behind: April 1937. / *D. W. K. Jones*

Right: It's that first Regent again with the last number. ST1139 stands unannounced with familiar crenellations towering behind, sometime after the war. / *John Fielder*

SOUTHASCOT ASCOT BUS & SH
MO 9320
148
BUS SERVICES
WHITE BUS SERVICES
JB 9468

ST 1139
LONDON TRANSPORT

Left: Occasionally red buses have helped work green routes. An example at Windsor in the early 1950s was STL1743, complete with the contemporary Country Department style of indicator information. / *Don Morris*

Below: With today's closure of Windsor Bridge to all motor traffic, route 445 through Eton to Datchet could no longer follow the same routeing. Once a Green Line coach, T654 of the 10T10 variety lost a little dignity on the short shuttle from the royal borough in about 1953. / *Don Morris*

Right: In March 1955, one of the other Windsor area independent operators, Blue Bus Service, continued to operate this Bedford with Beadle bus bodywork in appropriate livery on the route through Eton to Dorney with some journeys to Taplow now worked by Alder Valley through to Maidenhead. / *C. Carter*

Left: The five-bay construction and wide top deck front of Cravens bodywork for the RT is less apparent in the 1955 view of RT1422 with top deck window surrounds in green rather than the original cream. In the immediate postwar rush to replace worn out vehicles quickly, LT bought 120 Cravens-bodied RTs. The bodywork design was the fairly standard Cravens' offering with much detail modification to LT specification.

Now that letter suffixes are being avoided, route 457A via Upton Lea to Uxbridge is renumbered 452, previously familiar at the estuarine end of the Thames around Dartford and Greenhithe. / *C. Carter*

Below: Two of these Associated Daimler Co 424 coaches registered UC2217-18, spent rather idle lives as Green Line reliefs and on occasional private hire. Here's the second of them at Windsor in March 1935 trying its hand at local bus work. The sturdy bonnet and vee windscreen combine to give the vehicle a determined appearance. / *D. W. K. Jones*

Above: Leyland Cub C76B came from the People's Motor Services as the only one of the 106 members of the type to be acquired from an independent operator. It stands over one of Windsor garage's servicing pits in April 1937. / *D. W. K. Jones*

Left: On the threshold of Windsor garage, STL2066 takes up the sun while wearing trade plates towards the end of its Country bus life in about 1953. / *Don Morris*

Above right: At the same spot into the mid-1970s and long Routemaster bus RML2353 sports full National livery. / *Edward Shirras*

Right: Windsor's Green Line coach standards as planned for the 1950s (though facelifted for the late 1960s) and for the 1980s represented by RF28 and RB17 respectively. / *LCBS*

ROVE A DAY AWAY
GOLDEN ROVER
75p
457A
UXBRIDGE
BENTALLS BRACKNELL
LONDON COUNTRY
USED TICKETS
J·ISAACS
CUV 353C

PRIVATE
PAY AS YOU ENTER PLEASE
LYF 379
PRIVATE
GREEN LINE
PAY AS YOU ENTER PLEASE
PPH 447R

Bygone Slough

Above: The original minibus? Nippy Bus was the fleetname of this Morris-Commercial, registered RX3459, before the LPTB took it over and kept it on the Slough to Windsor run, as here in March 1935. / *D. W. K. Jones*

Below: This Gilford was one of the 20 or so normal control coaches converted after acquisition by LT to bus seating for one-man operation. This example worked from the then Slough garage (coded SL) in March 1935 on route 463 showing Belgrave Road. / *D. W. K. Jones*

Above: An elderly Maidstone & District open-top Leyland Titan TD1, equipped here in 1936 with an even older covered top from a withdrawn NS type bus, flogs out its last days in the extreme west of the LT area on a Slough local route. It had been numbered TD148B — as if, surely, it would have been 'C'! / *D. W. K. Jones*

Below: Slough station yard was a mecca for photographers in the 1930s. On the left of this 1936 line up was Q97, the youngest on parade. Between showers, driver and conductor discuss the receding merits of a former Maidstone & District Titan now TD138B, with its gruesome frontal aspect. The previously St Albans & District Tiger coach TR7B has arrived on the 441, and 442 to Farnham Royal is shown by C1, transferred from the Central Area. At this time it had a petrol engine, the experimental Perkins diesel unit having been removed. /*D. W. K. Jones*

Above: Working on route 441 between Windsor and Farnham Road's *George* in 1935 was TR1B, a bus which to later eyes looked remarkably reminiscent of the postwar red Mann Egerton-bodied Tiger PS1s. Before coming to LT in November 1934, this Tiger had been in the Reliance company's fleet and worked on route 50 in the Streatham area. / *D. W. K. Jones*

Below: A rarity was a single deck body on the Titan dd chassis, but here's one: ex-Robert Hawkins' TD86B, with a low-built rear entrance body settles down to work from Slough garage on route 335 after transfer from the Central Area in 1936. Thanks, conductor, for your characteristic pose with ticket rack and bell punch paraphernalia. / *D. W. K. Jones*

Above: After the war now, and good looking old timer T297 stands where Cubs stood prewar on route 442. Dolly stops show the rearrangements. The 458's road beyond Langley through Shreding Green and Iver was bedevilled by narrow lanes, sharp corners and beyond, by hump back bridges in those days, possibly explaining some of the dents and scratches in the otherwise smart appearance. Postwar livery was Lincoln green with white window frames, black lining above windows and wings, and matt brown roof. T297's radiator was painted too.

Below: During the early part of the war, the few single deckers that came from the provinces to alleviate the rolling stock shortage went mainly to the Country Department. This West Yorkshire Dennis Lancet served the Slough area. / *D. W. K. Jones*

In the Chiltern Hundreds

Left: Amersham garage's RLH46 shows a turn of speed on the verdant road to Uxbridge. Route 305, extended to the Middlesex market town in 1955, did not call for lowbridge buses — the 336 to Watford would have been a more expected allocation, but green RTs were in short availability in 1956.

Below: Fashionable ladies, old timers conversing on a bench and a crew looking back at Q71 on route 362C, which reached High Wycombe in 1937, combine to make an interesting study of the later 1930s. */ John Fielder*

Above: The Dennis Mace was the forward control version of the Guildford manufacturer's Ace. It was very rare in the LPTB fleet, only this one being acquired from Penn Bus Company whose No 32 it had been. It ran for a while from High Wycombe garage in the Penn livery of green and cream but was repainted and numbered DC3B in the same group as two Aces taking the earlier numbers. This picture was taken in September 1937. / *D. W. K. Jones*

Centre left: T382 was one of three AEC Regals with front entrances to originate with East Surrey. Here it is working a local route from High Wycombe before the war.

Below left: The width of roadway and forecourt combined to give unhindered opportunities for photography at Amersham garage through the years. This *circa* 1933 view of various types, including a Dennis EV (extreme right), and a Gilford AS6 next to it, captures the feel of the period, complete with petrol pumps, left. / *John Fielder*

Top: In the back of Amersham garage lurk two rather weary and unloved Tilling-Stevens Expresses registered UL7939-40, both from West London Coaches which used them on its London-Amersham-Aylesbury service. They were born in 1927, but by 1935 nobody seemed to have had a use for them. / *D. W. K. Jones*

Above: Green Line's route R had been Amersham & District's operation to London via the Chalfont villages and Uxbridge Road till October 1933. T366 waits for the garage clock to come up to departure time. The coach's front sidelights' position is noteworthy: mounted on the roof canopies either side of the indicators.

Above: STL2658 was one of the last chassis of the prewar Regent, being 'unfrozen' — manufacture completed for allocation to LT to meet wartime needs in 1942. The handsome body dates from before the war. Bodies for the unfrozen chassis came either from a random group of bodies undergoing repair at Chiswick works at the time or from any spares 'float' that was left. T671 looks on from behind. / *D. W. K. Jones*

Below: Amersham garage in 1949 was a photographer's dream; generally about half a dozen vehicles were lined up neatly on the broad forecourt extending the width of the old premises in this view and the new prewar-built garage seen in the previous photograph; standardisation had not cut the variety of types too deeply. The double-decker is STL2220, a Central Area bus with a wartime-built lowbridge body on a standard prewar chassis, transferred after the war to the Country Department from Harrow Weald garage. The three former Green Line Ts, 677, 678 and 521, were by now all in Country bus service; T677 shows a blind for route 394C while immediate sister alongside exhibits a well known lowbridge bus blind. / *D. W. K. Jones*

Above: Desperate shortages of buses led LT to negotiate the hire of brand new Bristols from provincial operators before delivery to them. A green lowbridge Bristol/Eastern Coach Works, already bearing its Hants & Dorset fleet number but not yet its fleet name, works on the 336 towards Amersham in 1950. / *D. W. K. Jones*

Left: Here at Chorleywood in 1948 is one of the two former Amersham & District Regents that became STs 1089-90 and continued for years on their original route, the 336./ *D. W. K. Jones*

Above right: For comparison, here's the twin, ST1089B, from the same angle, pictured before Chiswick had done occasional modifications. Sleet obscured the front windows one harsh prewar winter's day while the bus stops outside Chesham's Astoria cinema.

Right: Rakish T371B picks up at the same stop in drier weather for the 394 run to Chesham Moor.

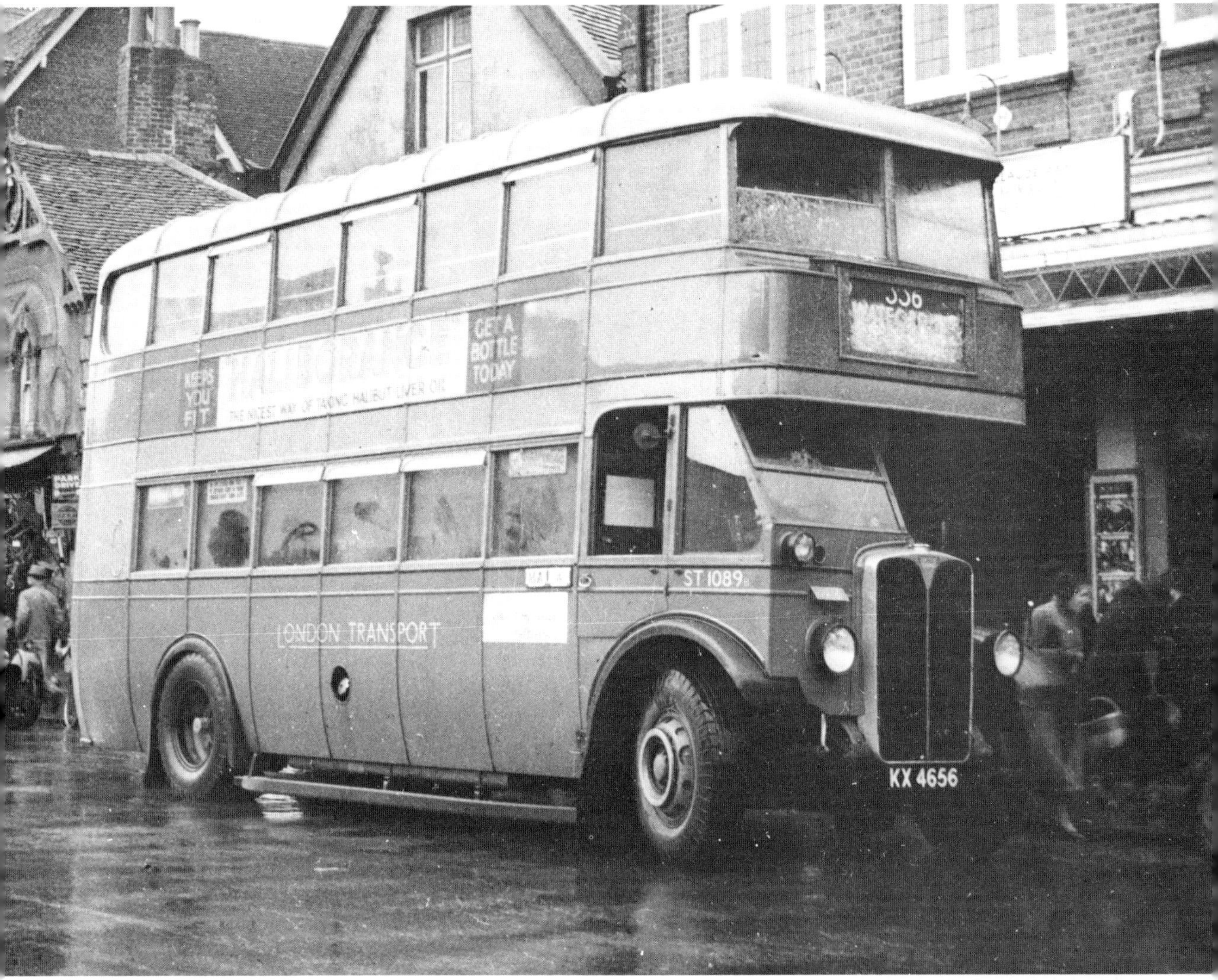
KEEPS YOU FIT
THE NICEST WAY OF TAKING HALIBUT LIVER OIL
GET A BOTTLE TODAY
LONDON TRANSPORT
ST 1089
KX 4656

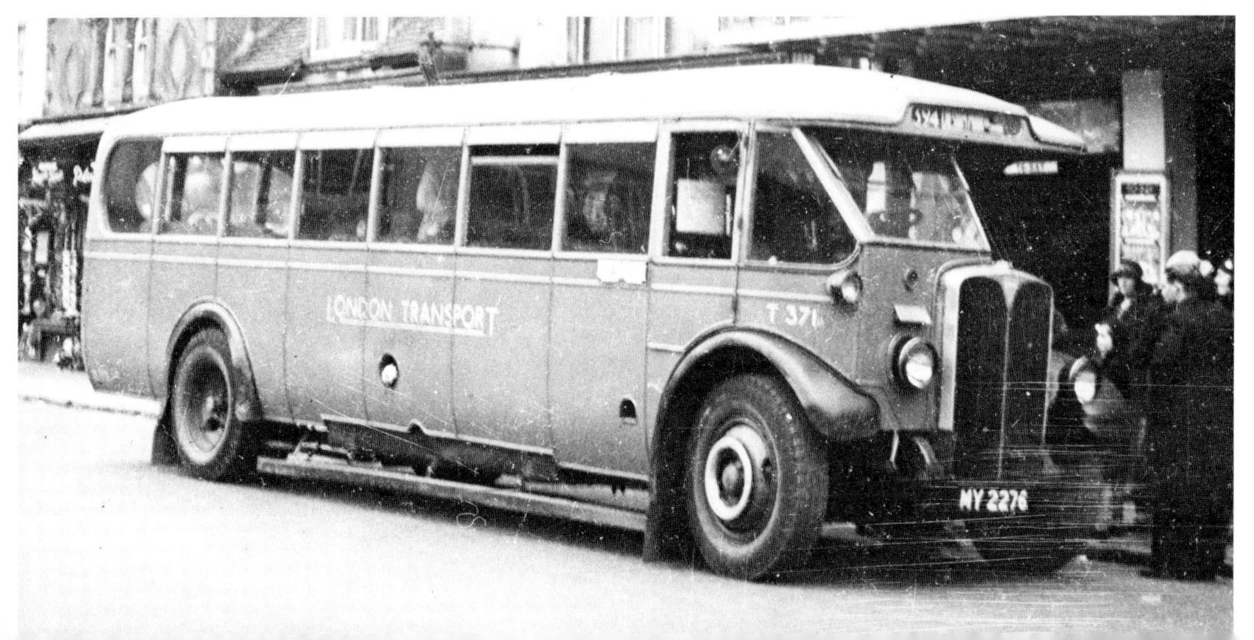

LONDON TRANSPORT
T 371
MY 2276

Above: A rare bird indeed was the photographer's thought as he tracked down (to Chesham, in May 1935) the only Dennis of its type to have come from Aldershot & District. It must have been one of the oldest-looking single-deckers to bear the London Transport fleetname. This route 359 to Hyde Heath was replaced by an extended 394 in 1942 and should not be confused with the later Eastern National-LT joint route with the same number from Amersham to Aylesbury. / *D. W. K. Jones*

Below: This Morris Viceroy was one of six buses with Park Royal bodywork to come to the LPTB from East Surrey/LGCS. With the small size fleetname and displaying route 397 Tring via Buckland Common, MS9B picks up outside the Broadway Tea Rooms where frequent tea costs 2d (rather less than 1p) and cycles are stored. / *D. W. K. Jones*

Above right: Chiltern summit in drizzling rain. Route 394 assumed the 397 journeys to Tring in 1968, giving a through, if circuitous, journey to Great Missenden. RF295 entices passengers out of the sturdy shelter in Tring in September 1969. / *C. Carter*

Right: Merlin MBS15, exchanged for LT's MBS4 in 1973, pictured in what were its familiar haunts: the picturesque village of Aldbury. / *LCBS*

394
GT. MISSENDEN STN
PAY AS YOU ENTER
PLEASE
NLE 514

387 ALDBURY &
TRING
LONDON COUNTRY
SMM 15F
School

301
LONDON TRANSPORT
UL 8972

TRING GARAG
BUS STOP
THE WORLDS CHOICE
ATKINSONS
EAU de COLOGNE
ST 1138.
LONDON TRANSPORT
UR 7879

Above left: Formerly owned by People's Motor Services of Ware, this old Gilford 1660T, GF169B, was one of the few half-cab versions in the LT fleet of Gilfords. Here it was warming up outside Two Waters garage, Hemel Hempstead, for the evening rush hour. / *D. W. K. Jones*

Left: ST1138 came from Lewis Omnibus Co of Watford and was later to receive a standard ST body. On route 301 to Tring, it draws away from the 'point' at Two Waters garage, the stop on this side of the road still having a provincial-style sign. / *D. W. K. Jones*

Above: One of Batten's fleet, Reliance R39C was first used as a coach by LT — the roof brackets can be seen — but it finished its days on bus work well away from earlier roads at Hemel Hempstead in about 1936. / *D. W. K. Jones*

Below: A bus built about 20 years later shows little outward difference in general appearance. This was the final form of the very long-running T type AEC Regals, descended from the earlier Reliance. T783, coded 15T13, with Mann Egerton bodywork, was in virtually new condition when caught by the camera between sun and shade at Hemel Hempstead in summer 1948. / *D. W. K. Jones*

Rickmansworth and Watford

Left: 'Provincial' was the epithet applied to the final and only postwar series of STLs: 2682-2701. Their composite Weymann bodies were very different from the LT standardised product, and crash gearboxes did not add to their popularity with staff. Despite this, most of them spent much of their time on the lengthy overlapping routes 321 and 351 with a great deal of stopping and starting between Luton and Rickmansworth and St Albans and Uxbridge respectively. STL2689 stands at the Rickmansworth station turning point that is now a car park in about 1949 before working a very short journey to Croxley Green. / *D. W. K. Jones*

Centre left: The close resemblance in rear end styles between the GS and RF types could be seen in the days when both ran from the stand in the cutting at Rickmansworth station. The old stand was above the bank behind the trees. GS33 warms up in March 1972 for a run on the short deviant 336A down to Loudwater. / *C. Carter*

Below left: Looking very muddy, numerically the last RF comes in from Berry Lane Estate just after London Country's birth in the month earlier. / *C. Carter*

Above right: Rickmansworth station in the last winter of the 1970s and Atlanteans are the double-deck rule. AN43 mounts the exit from the town centre and means to show number 321. / *John A. Gray*

Below right: Standard width Bristol BL23 waits on the downward slope of Rickmansworth station approach, seen from the top of the cutting, in March 1979. / *John A. Gray*

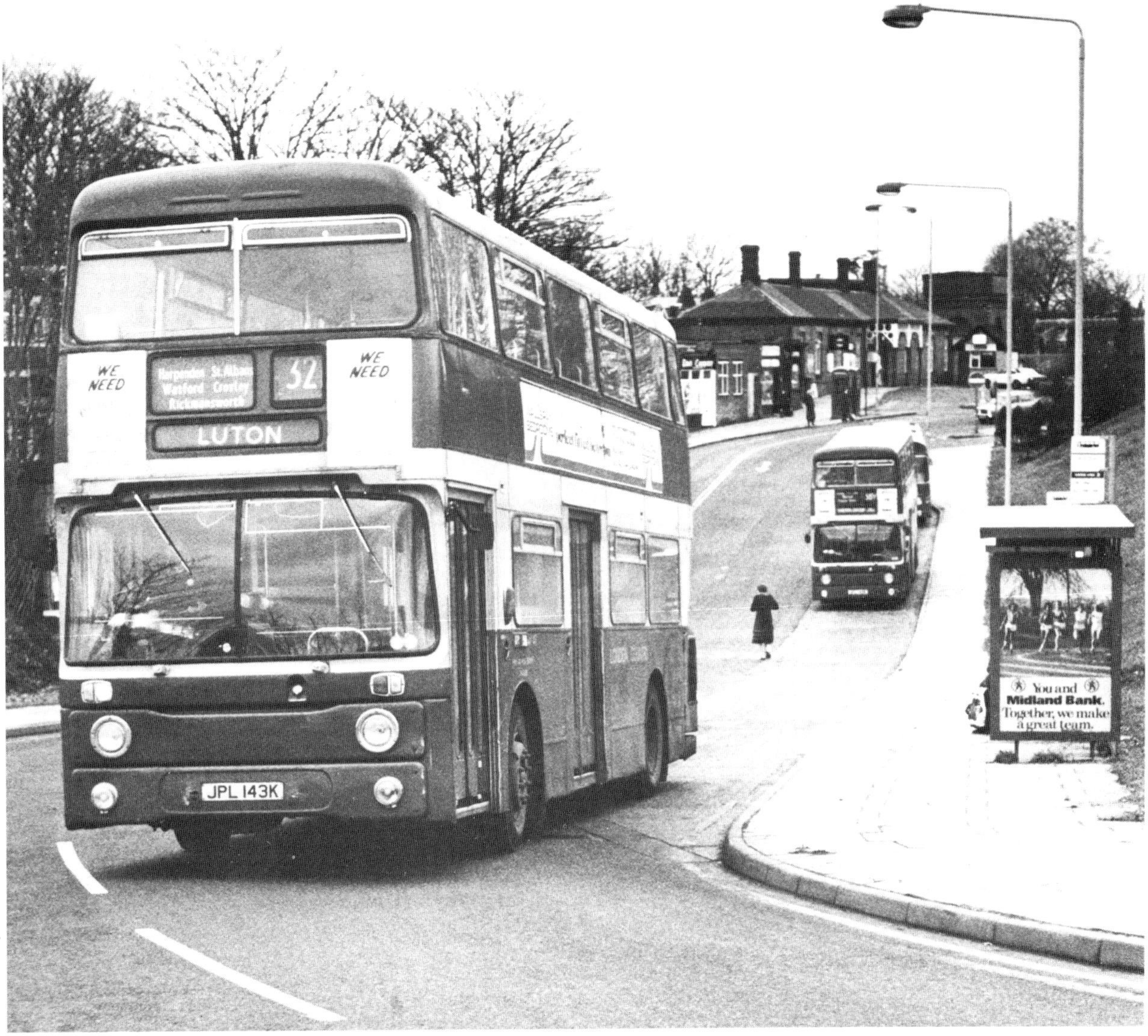
WE NEED
Harpenden St. Albans
Watford Croxley
Rickmansworth
32
WE NEED
LUTON
JPL 143K
You and
Midland Bank.
Together, we make
a great team.

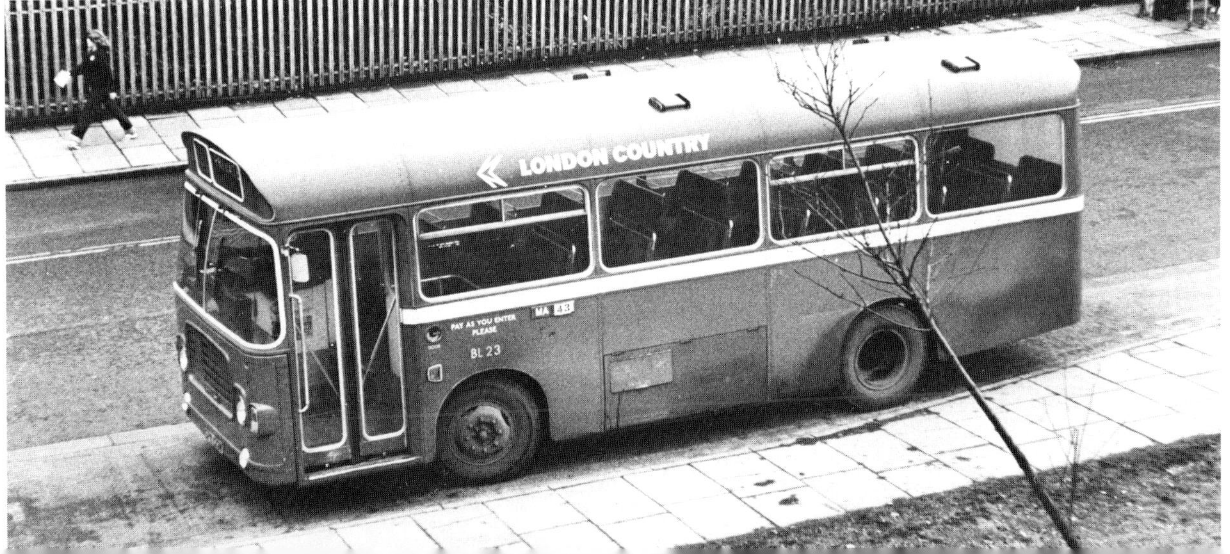

LONDON COUNTRY
PAY AS YOU ENTER
PLEASE
MA 43
BL 23

Above: Faithful RTs worked the 321 for many years. In February 1970, RT3867 climbs the cutting road out of Rickmansworth on a St Albans journey. Two panels have been undercoated to obliterate the LT fleetname. / *C. Carter*

Centre left: Lowbridge ST136, one of the group of eight STs (six from National and two from Amersham & District) with bodies designed to clear bridges on what became route 336, connects with the Metropolitan Line at Croxley Green station in the late 1940s before the station was renamed simply 'Croxley'. Met stations in Herts and Bucks were a model of harmony with the modest village building styles of the district. / *D. W. K. Jones*

Below left: Series B Leyland National SNB415 leaves New Road, Croxley Green, when doing a turn on the 321 while still very new in March 1979. Air vents replace the circular Leyland badge of the earlier series' front panelling, and a black bumper supersedes white, though still accommodating recessed foglights. The destination aperture had yet to be masked . . .

Above right: . . . at the back, the roof air intake hump has gone with the Series B.

Apart from much earlier renaming, Croxley station remains much the same as when the ST was photographed about 30 years earlier, though the stop flag has been changed to the new standard. / *John A. Gray*

Right: Despite two changes of ownership, this Albion in June 1934 was still serving the route for which it had been bought by the Metropolitan Railway in 1927: a feeder to Watford Met station. It came to LPTB by way of Lewis Omnibus Co controlled through a Metropolitan subsidiary whose chocolate livery and heterogeneous collection of vehicles were well known in the Hertfordshire area in the early 1930s. With its single headlamp, YU2974 was here painted green, black and white. / *D. W. K. Jones*

WATFORD WEST
GENERAL
YU 2974

321
BUY THE
DAILY
MIRROR
DAILY
WATFORD MARKET PL
WHIPPENDELL RD
CROXLEY GREEN
RICKMANSWORTH
GARSTON
LONDON TRANSPORT
GX 5315

UFOAM
PREMIER — ALBANIAN

Left: Busy activity around Watford post office not long before the war and 'Bluebird' ST1071 seems to be the centre of it, on the ever busy route 321. / *J. F. Higham*

Below left: Site preparation and early construction work for Watford's Town Hall underpass proceed apace as MBS276 waits to file through on route 346, followed by a van and then by an RP on its intended Green Line work. / *LCBS*

Above: Short and standard length Regents and one Q — all AECs built within a 16-year period, marshalled in the yard at Watford High Street garage in 1949. Coincidentally, all the double-deckers carry the *Picture Post* 'eyes' posters. From the left: STL2090; one of the 20 postwar STLs, minus its engine; STL1988; an engineless ST; Q44 looking unloved; STL1910; a Bluebird ST with at least its radiator missing; STL2615 which was later to be converted into SRT17 with a new RT body on its overhauled STL chassis for use in the Central Area; STL1989; STL2628 — later SRT55; STL1476 with front entrance bodywork, and STL1014 of the earlier front entrance kind with destination aperture below the route box. / *D. W. K. Jones*

Centre right: 'Bluebird' was the name commonly given to the STs of this design built at Chiswick for London General Country Services Ltd in 1932. The nickname probably stemmed from the pleasing interior decor in shades of blue. By 1949, this member of the batch registered in Surrey, ST1039, was nearing the end of its days and relegated to driving instruction duties at Watford. / *D. W. K. Jones*

Right: There were 50 Weymann-bodied STLs like this, very similar to 89 earlier ones with Chiswick bodywork. All were Country buses. STL1490 appears here in all Lincoln green with cream relief, upper windows included, but the prewar green and white produced a strikingly effective livery for this design. / *D. W. K. Jones*

Above right: Veterans parade. ST884, ex-Tilling and retaining red livery on its sagging body work, lines up with ST1094, ex-East Surrey and with squared cab, at High Street yard in 1949. Some indicators in those hard up days were vestigial — not much better than today, but with more excuse. / *D. W. K. Jones*

Centre right: Newly delivered RT968 with Weymann bodywork stands on the tarmac at Watford High Street garage. Wartime abbreviated indicator standards still prevailed. / *D. W. K. Jones*

Below: Relief coaches were still on hire into 1951 in Watford. The junction station clock shows 1.25 on a cold February day that year as a Bunty Coaches' Leyland Tiger PS1 picks up passengers bound for the St. Albans and Luton direction. A Cravens-bodied RT draws up behind as one of the postwar STLs moves towards the town centre in the opposite direction. / *D. W. K. Jones*

Above: Watford Junction on a dim winter's afternoon 28 years later: an Atlantean, different street lighting, three transport logos, but the same station clock. / *John A. Gray*

Left: AN49 could have accommodated the suffix in route number 385A without renumbering it to 389, a cross-Watford local route. The laden bus leaves the junction station in March 1979. / *John A. Gray*

St Albans and Beyond

Above: Route 321 and its predecessors are constants in the north western area.

One of 30 coaches formerly operated by Hill's Strawhatter Coaches of Luton, this unusual centre-entrance Gilford 168OT was relegated to Country bus duties by LT, though for once in a home area. In July 1934 it was at Harpenden on a St Albans to Luton run. / *D. W. K. Jones*

Right: Country postwar Regent STL2693 on the 351 meets a hired red Bristol of Eastern Counties working Central Area route 84 — the long tentacle — on St Albans garage forecourt in 1950. / *D. W. K. Jones*

Above: Twenty years on and RT4044 works the linked successor route 321 southwards past St Peter's Church and the war memorial in St. Albans. Despite February's temperatures, in 1970 short skirts were fashionable and a day out with a Green Rover ticket cost a mere eight shillings (40p). */ LCBS*

Right: Buses on route 321 could display more route information than most, in view of the route's length and important centres served. New AN159 chooses to show only half of Harpenden when working through St Albans in a winter 1979 snow flurry on one of the hourly short journeys from Rickmansworth. */ John A. Gray*

Left: The red bus on the 84 in 1979 is Daimler Fleetline DMS1894, with foglights beaming on a dismal January day. For company it has overhauled SMW13. The AEC Swifts bodied by Marshall's of Cambridge are the longest London Country examples of the Swift type; at about 36ft 6in, a little longer even than Merlins. / *John A. Gray*

Centre left: Central Area Q179 with Park Royal bodywork was one of a small number lent to the Country Department in 1937. The route number stencil above the driver's side window was in use, for once. Painted green, the side-engined bus stands on the garage forecourt in front of the evergreen tree and the London Transport flagpole. / *D. W. K. Jones*

Below: It's February 1972 and though the evergreen remains, the economy pole carries a changed symbol as SMW15, a Swift that came from South Wales Transport about six months earlier, pulls off the forecourt for a short 343 journey. / *C. Carter*

Right: Unlike the earlier overhauls of the Marshall-bodied Swifts that had their beading and badges removed, SMW8, at St Albans garage in January 1979, still keeps these features, though painted over. / *John A. Gray*

Below right: LT1137, the Green Line AEC Renown with experimental bodywork (perhaps the ultimate in the voguish 'piano front' style) had been demoted to bus work from Hatfield garage by the time it was photographed on route 330 in St Albans in April 1935. It has only one of its two front display areas in use. The other formerly had a Green Line sign, capable of being lit. / *D. W. K. Jones*

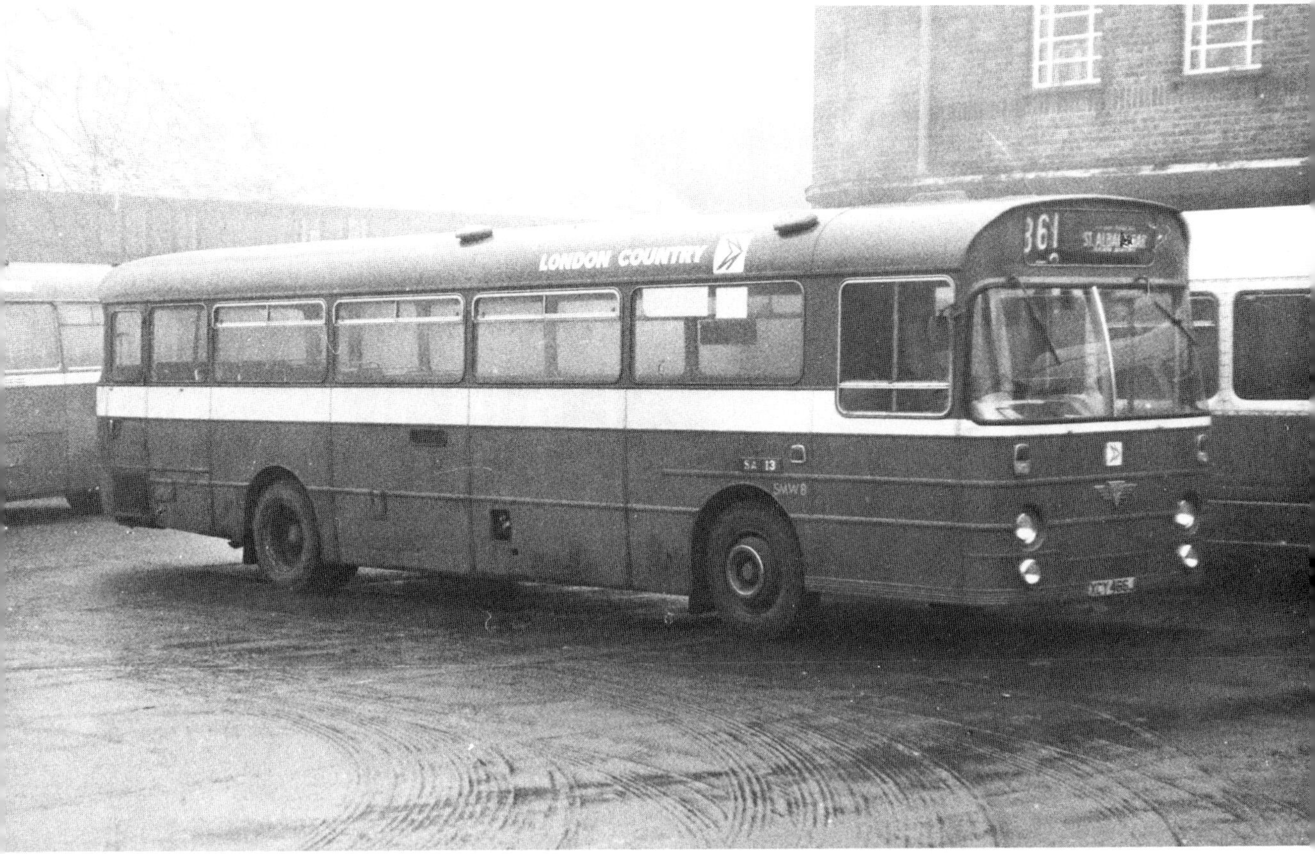

LONDON COUNTRY
361
SA 13

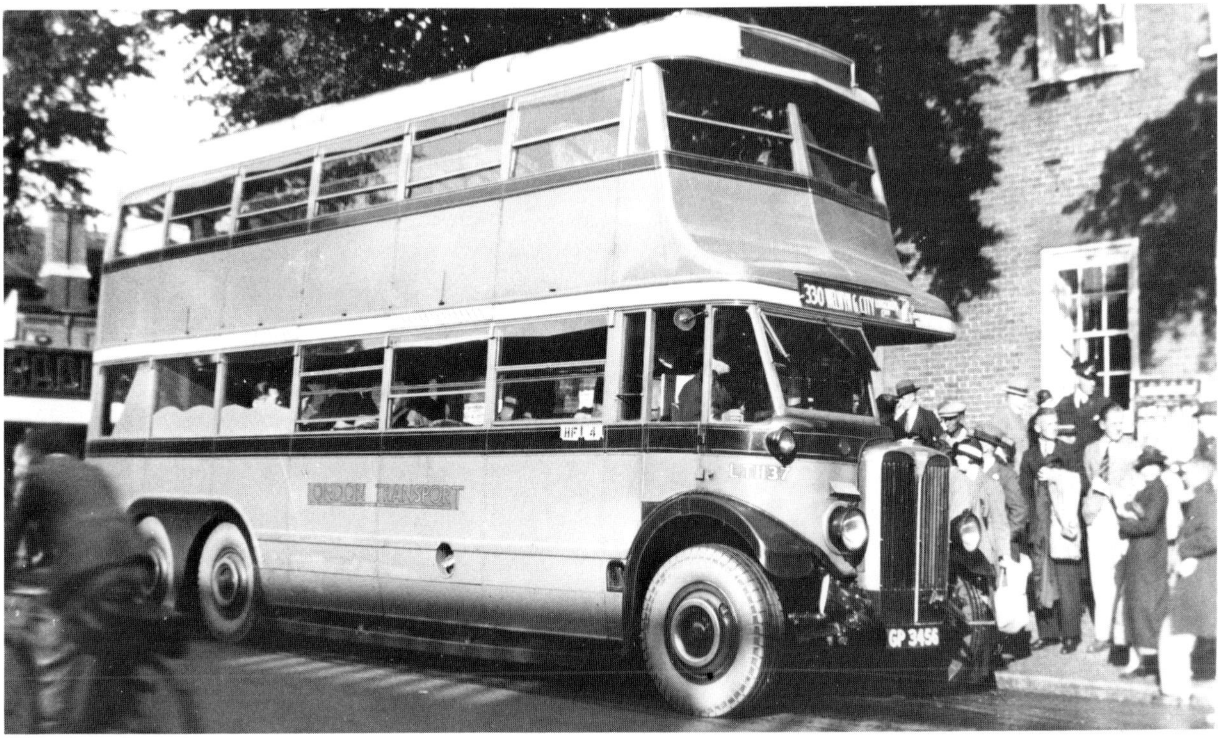

HF 4
LONDON TRANSPORT
GP 3456

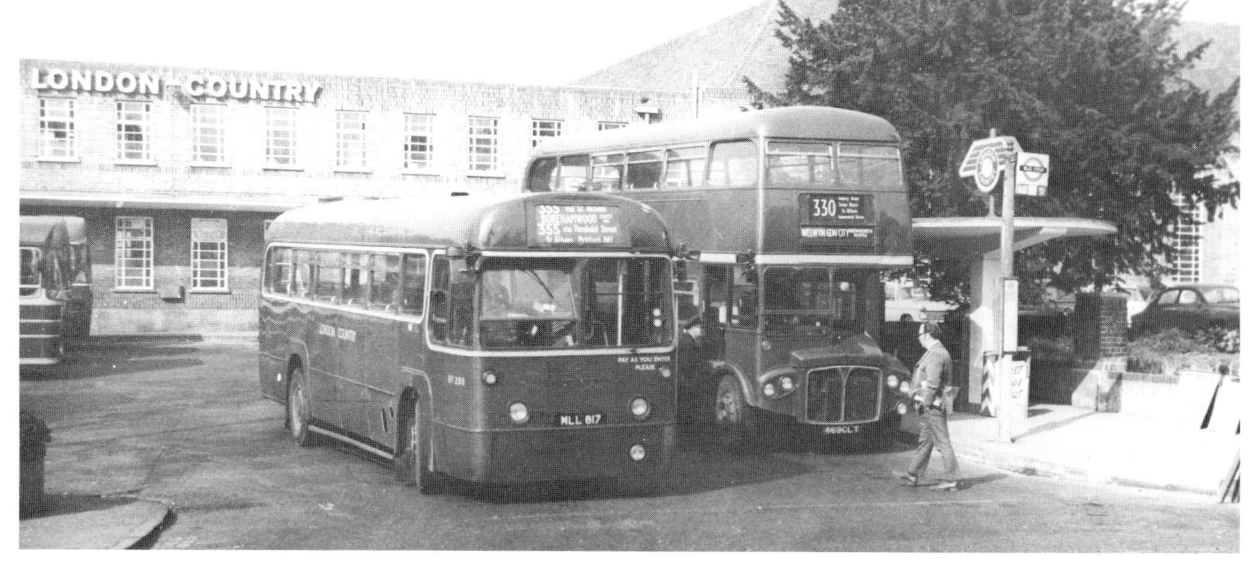

LONDON COUNTRY
BOREHAMWOOD
355
330
WELWYN GARDEN CITY
LONDON COUNTRY
PAY AS YOU ENTER PLEASE
MLL 817
469CLT

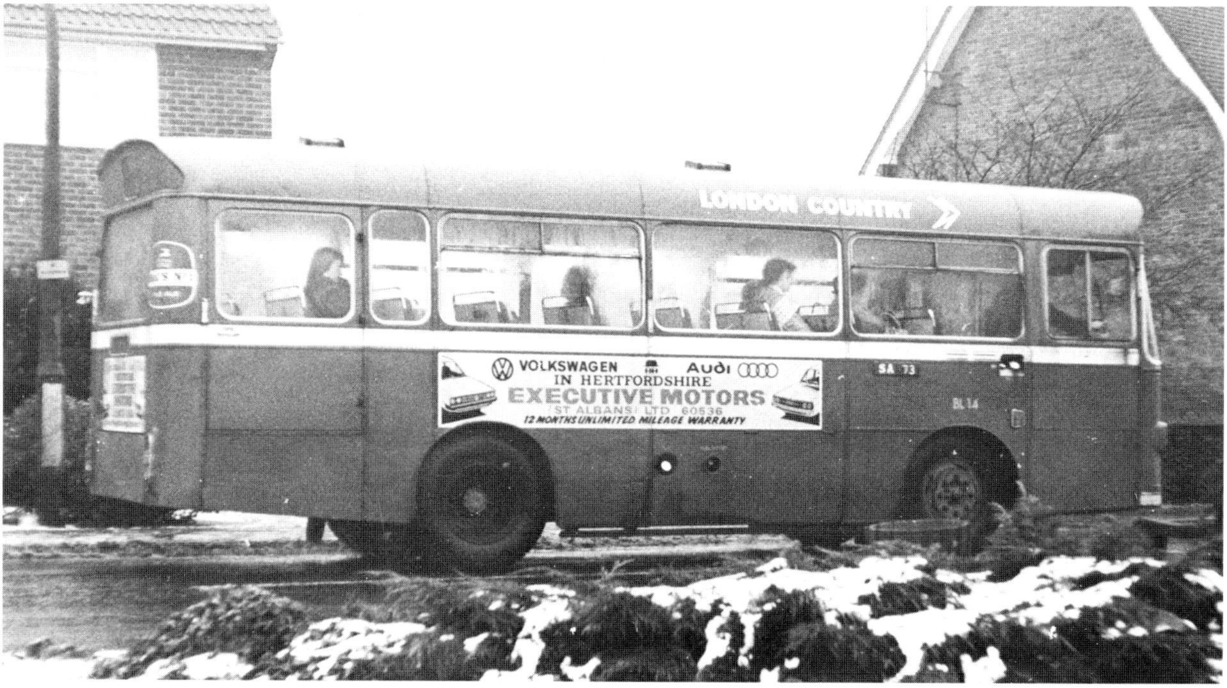
LONDON COUNTRY
VOLKSWAGEN Audi
IN HERTFORDSHIRE
EXECUTIVE MOTORS
(ST ALBANS) LTD 60536
12 MONTHS UNLIMITED MILEAGE WARRANTY

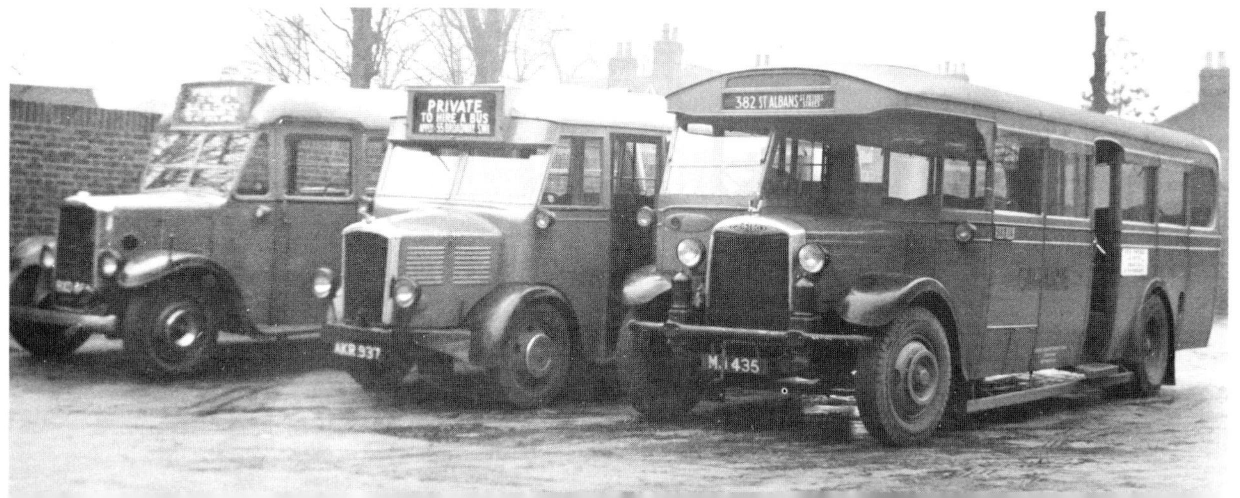

PRIVATE
TO HIRE A BUS
382 ST ALBANS
AKR 537

Top left: Route 330 had RMC1469 for contemporary comfort to Welwyn Garden City in 1972. Alongside, RF280 shows a mixture of route 355 information; presumably the aperture should have been partly masked. / *C. Carter*

Centre left: Route 355 further north, at Sandridge, in snowtime. Bristol LHS6L BL14 pulls away for the uphill ride to St Albans one January 1979 Saturday. The steamy windows could show the effectiveness of the heaters in the Eastern Coach Works' 35-seat body. / *John A. Gray*

Left: Outside St Albans garage in February 1937 the line up includes one of the new Leyland Cubs; a 'flying pig' — Dennis Ace, and Gilford GF92 from Strawhatter of Luton showing a blind for the 382, a route still running similarly today. / *D. W. K. Jones*

Top: Square grilles were featured on some of the Qs with bodywork built by the Birmingham Railway Carriage & Wagon Co. Q91 stands outside the garage in the fine summer of 1948. / *D. W. K. Jones*

Above: The AEC demonstrator registered UMP227 was attached to St Albans garage in April 1950. It was the prototype for the highly successful and enduring Regal Mk IV of which LT bought 715 examples, the last of which left revenue earning service in 1979. UMP227 carried an approximation of standard green livery, but of course no fleetname or number since AEC Ltd remained the owner. / *D. W. K. Jones*

Above: The 1979 winter's darkness begins to close in on the garage so that yellow training Leyland Titan PD3/4 LR17 loses a little of its bright identity. Penultimate Merlin, MBS437, could do with a thorough wash. / *John A. Gray*

Left: A London Transport staff bus takes a rest, framed by a way into the back of the garage: January 1979. Once a member of the 65-strong batch of BEA Routemasters used to ferry air passengers between West London Air Terminal and the London airports, notably Heathrow, RMA18 came into LT ownership when demand for the airports service fell in the mid-1970s. Here in usual Routemaster livery, the vehicle is clearly different from its bus sisters in having no provision for a route information display. Less obvious minor differences are the one-piece windscreen and headlamp and 'hemline' arrangements in the style of London Country's RCLs. / *John A. Gray*

Above right: St Albans' main north-south thoroughfare is the shop- and tree-lined St Peter's Street. This early picture shows a Leyland Lion numbered L1 in the fleet of The Express Motor Service. / *John Fielder*

Right: Bedford BD8B worked at Purfleet before acquisition by LPTB, who allocated it to local routes in the St Albans area. Here it shows a blind for the 338 to London Colney. Like most Bedfords it had a short life before passing to an independent operator; few lasted after the introduction of the standard Leyland Cubs in 1935-36. / *D. W. K. Jones*

CAFE
ST. ALBANS
The Express

PLEASE
BE CAREFUL
LONDON TRANSPORT
AMY 660

Above: Formerly owned by Colne, Gilford GF145B was one of the few left to work in its home area, here about to leave St Albans on route 343 for Colney Heath in October 1935. / *D. W. K. Jones*

Below: St Peter's Street more recently. Green Line orbital route 724 had been cut back from Romford to Harlow in spring 1978, hence Harlow is the (small!) destination shown by Duple-bodied Reliance RB48 early in the following year. / *John A. Gray*

Towns New and Old: Stevenage and Hitchin

Top: Stevenage is a town singled out by having Country buses in other than the usual contemporary green livery. Right at the end of 1969 LT introduced a 'guaranteed bus' service — Blue Arrow — for workpeople, running close to their homes and work places mornings, lunchtimes and evenings. Fleetline XF6 was one of three specially repainted light blue and white to work the service which was later eclipsed by the success of Superbus. / *C. Carter*

Above: Superbus livery — chrome yellow and bright blue — as applied to overhauled Swift SM487, now in September 1978 with the London Country fleetname and National symbol as well as the SB motif. / *John A. Gray*

Above: Metro-Cammell-bodied Swift SM520 was a comparative newcomer to Stevenage Superbus work when pictured in autumn 1978. On its recent overhaul the bus had received the National Bus Co corporate green and white livery and a change in registration number plate style to the reflective variety.

Swift can be distinguished frontally from close sister Merlin by its two foglamps; Merlins have just the nearside one. / *John A. Gray*

Below: Four Metro-Scanias were purchased for the Superbus routes in 1971-72, and three more came secondhand in 1973 to join them. These partly Swedish-built buses look quite distinctive and their deep nearside windscreen is a unique feature. / *LCBS*

Right: Atlanteans salute. AN39 on town route 801 in September 1978 wears 'light' National green and yellow but with the later corporate fleetname style while AN12 beyond in similar colours carries the Superbus initials while working on the SB2. / *John A. Gray*

Below right: The old town of Stevenage forms the backdrop for RT3510 in September 1970 while the bus passed through on a route 800 journey. / *C. Carter*

TOWN SERVICE
07
SB
AN39 SV
TRY
Be assured for life 
LONDON and MANCHESTER ASSURANCE
CIRCULAR VIA BEDWELL
800
STEVENAGE
LYR 929

Top: Route number 800A is difficult to discern on the front display of later type Atlantean AN131, which has only a single doorway and front staircase. / *John A. Gray*

Above: Route 379 runs only on certain days, and then infrequently. Narrow Bristol LH BN47 makes an appearance at Stevenage bus station one Saturday afternoon in September 1978; passing the third kind of single-decker to operate as a Superbus — Leyland National; in this case, LN23. / *John A. Gray*

Above: Atlantean AN12 leads AN69 out of Danesgate into the short length of Danestrete to attain Stevenage's temporarily quiet bus station in 1978. Mann Egerton, advertised on AN12's engine bustle, is now a burgeoned car distributor, but built London single deck bus bodies in a modest way just after the war. / *John A. Gray*

Below: Park Royal Vehicles, long noted as a major builder of London's double-deck bodywork, turned a hand to 90 single-deck bodies for Reliance chassis in 1971-72. The ensuing RPs took over Green Line work from Routemasters, though by 1978 some RPs were themselves beginning to slide down the status scale to be buses in the Stevenage area. In September though RP7 continued on Green Line work, here picking up a breathless passenger in Danestrete for a 732 express journey. / *John A. Gray*

Above: Non standards — all in yellow liveries — languish behind Stevenage garage in autumn 1978. Partly seen on the left is MS4, the Metro-Scania type CR111MH we met just now. Behind the car is one of the 20 Leyland Titan PD3/4s acquired secondhand in 1975-76 for use of training drivers. With its back to us is another Metro-Scania, this time a model BR111, but still with Metro-Cammell 45 seats plus 15 standing bodywork. LCBS came by MS6 and two sisters in autumn 1973 after they had worked from new in the Winchester area for Chisnell's King Alfred services and, after take-over, for Hants & Dorset. In front of a third MS stands another ex-Ribble Titan trainer, LR20. The forwardmost lower deck side window was put in after staircase removal to permit driving instruction. / *John A. Gray*

Left: Seen at Stevenage garage: Atlantean reflections over a pit . . .

Below: . . . and dolly textures. / *both John A. Gray*

Left: The photographer tries not to disturb RT3046 contemplating its destiny, neglected at the back of Stevenage garage in September 1978. / *John A. Gray*

Below: Let's have an RT still in shining paintwork and complete with rear hub covers on New Year's Day 1972 to take us north to Hitchin on the 801 — hardly a 'Town Service' as proclaimed by the route blind. / *C. Carter*

Below: Women shoppers look vainly for an absent driver to open LN21's front doors so that they may sit and rest. The bus stop flags in St Mary's Square are now the standard ones, carried on erstwhile London Transport posts. Route 300 was so renumbered from 303A to avoid the suffix. However, in September 1978, route 303C still continued, as evidenced by the stop flag. / *John A. Gray*

Right: Route 303A in its Routemaster days: September 1969. RMC1500, still with Green Line ephemera applied, prepares to leave for New Barnet, no longer served by London Country buses. / *Tom Maddocks*

Below right: The prototype Routemaster coach at the same spot, for comparison. The conductor has a smoke and a chat to his driver of RMC4, the only Routemaster with Eastern Coach Works bodywork, at Stevenage bus station in September 1970. / *C. Carter*

MITED
303A
NEW BARNET STN
KRAZY KETTLE
500 CLT
303
NEW BARNET STN
HARDY & C
SLT 59

Bygone Barnet

Left: The other end of route 303 in the early LT days had this former National and LGCS NS1033 working out of Hatfield garage at New Barnet station in April 1935. The route number stencil is discernible between the destination board and the roof. A lamp housed in the box central on the cab canopy lit the whole display.

One of the peculiarities of the Country Department early on was the haphazard application of fleet numbers: even when allocated they were less often applied on the offside. */ D. W. K. Jones*

Centre left: ST1063 of another type to work the 303, was one of the few to receive its fleet number in black when a comprehensive numbering scheme became evident in 1935 in the Country Area. With its tiny door, the driver's cab side at least had minimal protection from bad weather. */ D. W. K. Jones*

Bottom left: This Gilford was from Edward Hillman, working here from Hertford garage. Its Green Line transfers may indicate a coach but its fleet number, GF149B, signified a bus. Anomalies of this sort were frequent well beyond September 1935 when this picture was taken at New Barnet station. */ D. W. K. Jones*

Above right: The Lewis Omnibus Co alone supplied the small Bristol element in the LPTB fleet in 1933. This example, in the early black and green livery, was working through period suburbia at East Barnet in winter 1935. */ D. W. K. Jones*

Right: Bovril posters link Town and Country at New Barnet station. Note the square cab and flush indicator of the former East Surrey ST1128 at left. It would have been a slow journey by ST from Watford to Victoria, but at least only one change of bus was needed, on to ST812 . . . */ D. W. K. Jones*

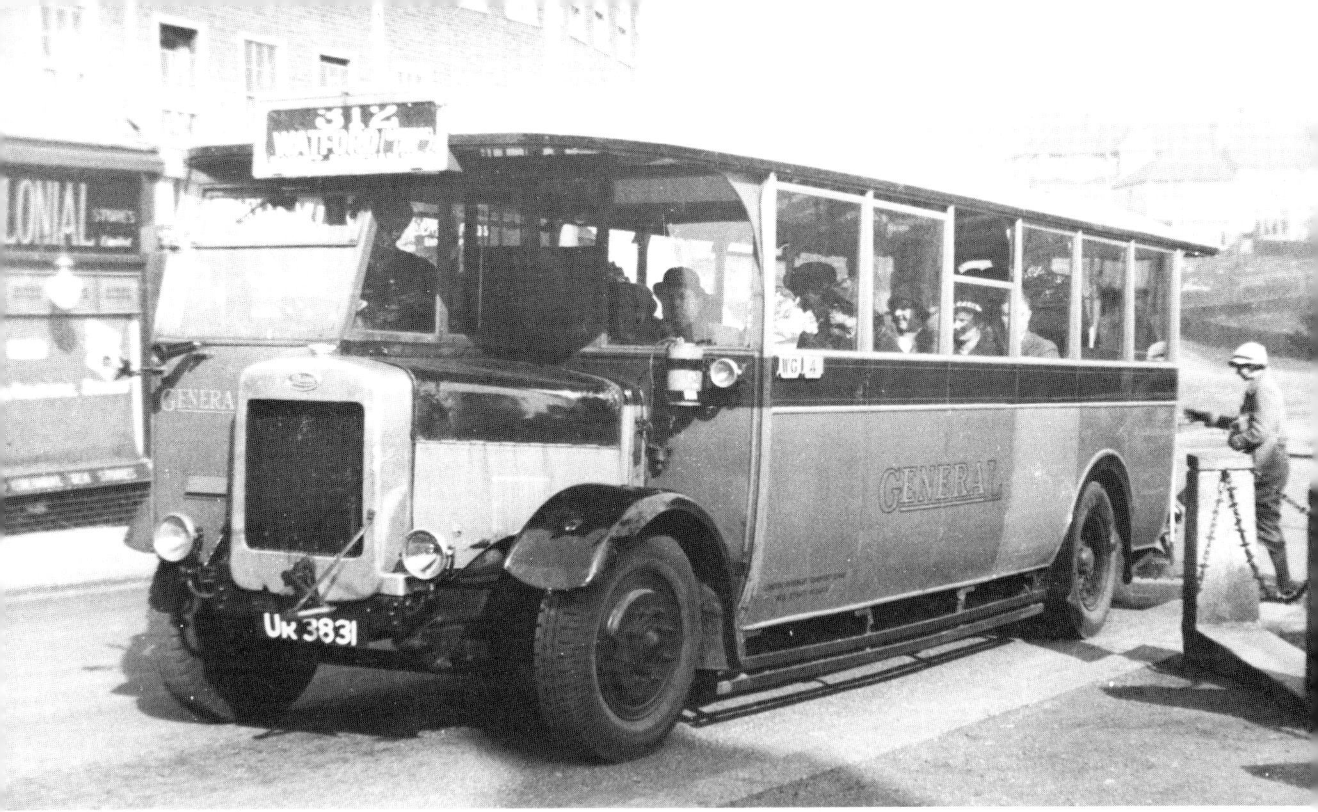
312
GENERAL
UK 3831

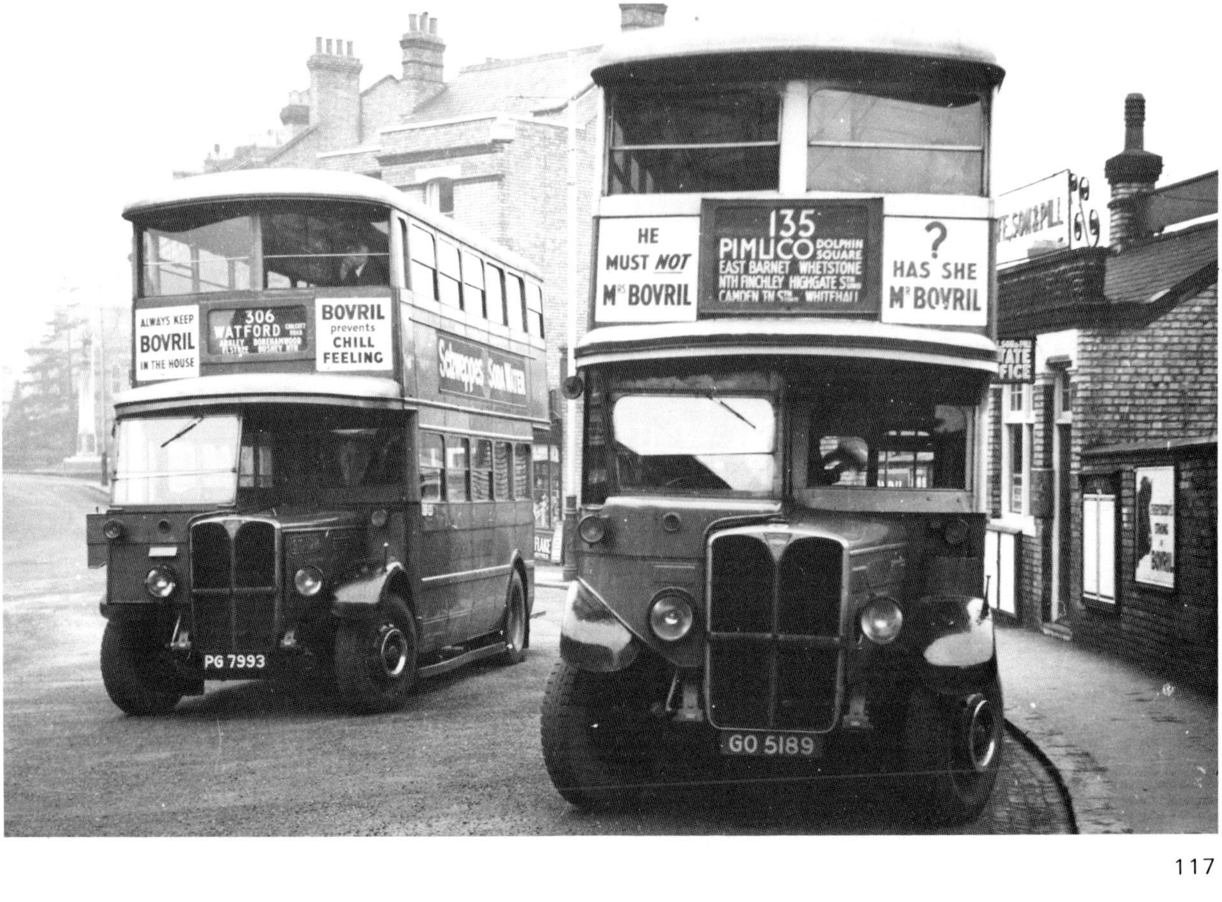
ALWAYS KEEP
BOVRIL
IN THE HOUSE
306
WATFORD
BOVRIL
prevents
CHILL
FEELING
Schweppes SODA WATER
PG 7993
HE
MUST NOT
Mrs BOVRIL
135
PIMLICO DOLPHIN SQUARE
EAST BARNET WHETSTONE
NTH FINCHLEY HIGHGATE Stn
CAMDEN TN Stn WHITEHALL
?
HAS SHE
Mr BOVRIL
GO 5189

Hertford, and into Essex

Left: This veteran Bristol B came all the way from Darlington to Hertford garage to relieve the rolling stock shortage in 1940. The crew was happy to pose, less happy with their slogging monster on Hertfordshire hills. / *D. W. K. Jones*

Below: Another bus to venture away from its first home area was Surrey-registered Regal T84B. Route 379 is the present counterpart to the old 329 whose country terminus was Nup End.

Top: No mention of Hertford would be complete without including a Cub on the town route 333 to Bengeo. C38 obliges here outside *The Woolpack* in 1952. / *Don Morris*

Above: This just prewar version of the Leyland Tiger was a production pioneer of the underfloor position in the 1950s. TF84 came numerically towards the end of the batch of 75 Chiswick-bodied Green Line coaches, nearly all of which finished their London lives as service buses. Photographed at Hertford bus station in about 1952. / *Don Morris*

Above: Central Area veteran RT128, its prewar-designed Chiswick bodywork repainted green in this 1956 picture, stands alongside youthful Guy Special GS12 (which we've met before at Crawley) at Hertford bus station, while a couple chat engagingly. The first batch of RTs were light enough to cross a weak bridge on route 327; the postwar version was a bit too heavy.
/ *D. W. K. Jones*

Below: By November 1972, RF286 was working route 327. Dirt on the bus was not so thick as to obscure the fleetname in an unusual position, presumably applied there to permit an advertisement to be pasted in the usual fleetname place. / *C. Carter*

Left: Route 393 was the first introduction to serve the infant new town of Harlow, and it was worked by the faithful Leyland Cub from Epping garage. Here in April 1952, C74 comes by RT1017 on the established trans-Harlow 396 route.

Below: The first of London Country's production Atlanteans, AN1, leaves Harlow bus station in June 1974 displaying the exact fare notice for the town's flat fare routes.
/ *Tom Moore*

Left: Harlow tried a minibus service for two years based on the concept of the passenger telephoning a central control requesting the bus to stop near his home on a specified journey. Ford Transit FT1 performed the service in October 1974, a couple of months after the introduction of the facility, novel in the London Country area. With room for 16 seated passengers, the Dormobile bodywork had a livery of National green and white with the pick-me-up labels in black on yellow. / *C. Carter*

Below: RT1024 stands in its prime on the forecourt of Epping garage in June 1950 with a few minutes to go before leaving for Bishop's Stortford on a 396 journey. Epping garage was later replaced by a new garage at Harlow. / *C. Carter*

Right: Among the RTs on Epping's forecourt in May 1952 was — STL773, about to take a turn on the 396. This old girl had come over from Luton: J. W. Green's ales advertised on the side, as a local Luton brew, may have meant little to people in Epping, Sawbridgeworth or Stortford. / *C. Carter*

Below right: Back a year to 1951 to have a look at the Tiger FEC coach in its intended Green Line role. TF31 picks up outside Epping's *George & Dragon* for the southwards run to Aldgate. / *C. Carter*

BP
SHELL
CHUNKY
MARMALADE
J.W. GREEN'S ALES
EPPING
BXD 432

EARCE
OVIS
LUNCHEONS
TEAS
HOVIS
720
LONDON
SHEPHERD.
GEORGE &
DRAGON
FJJ 642

The Detached East

Left: Edward Hillman operated a large fleet of Gilfords on routes from east London. No 124, one of his latest 168OT coaches, bears Green Line transfers on its striking blue, black and white livery as it stands outside the former Hillman garage at Romford in 1934. */ D. W. K. Jones*

Below: The Romford-Tilbury district of the Country Area was self-contained for bus operation, with no routes linking other green bus routes in the rest of the area. Probably the longest route in the detached portion is still the 370, here worked by TD52. After acquisition, some Central Area Titans were transferred to the Country Department, and this former Pioneer Omnibus Company example was one of them, allocated to Grays garage. */ D. W. K. Jones*

Top: The northern orbital Green Line route 724 has had its termini changed at both ends since this August 1970 photograph at Romford station. Heathrow Airport is the substitute for High Wycombe at the western end, and coaches terminate short at Harlow now on eastbound journeys. RF37 received bodywork restyling in the late 1960s, and lasted for another four years after this picture. / *Tom Maddocks*

Above: An isolated route was Rainham to Rainham Ferry, all the way for 1d (less than $\frac{1}{2}$p) at once upon a time. Bedford BD5 ex-Enterprise (Fletcher), Gravesend, works out the last of its LPTB life on 375 in 1937. / *D. W. K. Jones*

Above: In September 1951, the Country Department took responsibility for working some Eastern National routes in the Grays/Tilbury area. Pictured on the first day, 30th, is a Bristol J type of Eastern National with LT fleetname already applied, standing at a newly-erected LT stop at Grays war memorial. The destination was Bulphan; passengers were left to presume it was on route 44. / *C. Carter*

Centre left: The Eastern National vehicles were left in that company's green and cream livery while running for LT. This Bedford OB, EN No 3929, carries the standard London Transport fleetname and running number stencil holders. The women must have wondered if there'd be room for them in this already crowded small capacity bus. / *D. W. K. Jones*

Below left: Some EN double-deckers too worked for LT for a few months till RTs supplanted them. One of them was this angular-looking wartime lowbridge Guy. / *D. S. Giles*

Above right: Grays Eastern National garage looks little changed on 1 October 1951 after operational transfer to the Country Department. Five formidable looking prewar Dennis Lancets and a wartime Guy Arab form the rank. / *D. W. K. Jones*

Right: STL1928 was drafted in time for work on hitherto Eastern National route 37A on the first day, here at Grays. / *C. Carter*

3879
JTW 234

GRAYS
CONSERVATIVE
CLUB
White Label
TILBURY FERRY
37A
AND
GRAYS
DLU 287

Right: In August, 1969, RT4746 was leaving Grays for Romford on route 370, which had been linked with Eastern National's 37A in January 1952 to form a through facility. */ C. Carter*

Below: The contemporary counterpart at Grays is the Bristol VRT rear-engined double-decker with Eastern Coach Works bodywork as supplied to many members of the National Bus Company. BT2 demonstrates its lines when new in spring 1977. */ LCBS*